THE
FIRST ENGLISH TRANSLATORS
OF THE CLASSICS

THE
FIRST ENGLISH TRANSLATORS
OF THE CLASSICS

BY
C. H. CONLEY, Ph.D.

KENNIKAT PRESS, INC./PORT WASHINGTON, N. Y.

CONTENTS

ACKNOWLEDGMENTS

Thɪs study was presented in its original form to the Faculty of Yale University in partial fulfilment of the requirements for the doctor's degree. It has since been re-written, new material has been incorporated, and a number of the passages taken from works belonging to the sixteenth century have been compared with the first editions. Grateful acknowledgment is made to Professor J. M. Berdan for suggesting the subject of this investigation and for giving much encouragement and helpful criticism during its earlier stages. Professor W. E. Mead, with whom the author has been associated in the same college department for a period of years, has been kind enough to read some of the galleys.

THE
FIRST ENGLISH TRANSLATORS
OF THE CLASSICS

INTRODUCTION

IN view of the amount of scholarly effort from first to last expended upon earlier Tudor and late Elizabethan literature, the scant attention usually paid to the output of the initial years of the Good Queen's reign is somewhat surprising. Preceding the great Elizabethans by scarcely a generation, the writers of the sixties might be expected to call forth considerable interest from students of sixteenth century English literature. Yet between Surrey and Spenser there at present exists a real hiatus in our scholarship. The majority of works dealing with English literature of the period, many of them otherwise carefully done, at this point suddenly become curiously vague. Of course, comparatively little original writing was produced for a score of years after the disorders of Edward's and Mary's times, yet the numerous translations—in most cases the first renditions into English of the several works—are deserving of careful study,[1]

[1] Among recent systematic attempts to treat the early Elizabethan translations from the classics, Whibley's chapter in the *Cambridge History of English Literature* (Volume 4, Chapter I), comprehending the whole reign, contains much excellent, more or less general description and appreciation; and Miss Amos' chapter (*Early Theories of Translation*, Chapter III), which covers the whole sixteenth century, consists of a compilation of the translators' opinions on various selected topics. No one seems to have undertaken to examine the causes which led to the early translating activity or to have recognized the difficulties encountered by the first translators. As for students of texts, Immelmann (*von Surrey's Aeneis*, 1905 *Jahrbuch der Deutschen Shakespeare Gesellschaft* XLI), Fest (*Ueber Surrey's Virgilübersetzung*, 1904), and Brenner (*Thomas Phaer's Aeneis-Uebersetzung*, 1912) have confined their attention chiefly to philological and metrical matters. De Vocht has

especially since the classics in the original, generally considered conducive of culture and freedom of thought, in the sixteenth century, as will be shown, served to defeat liberal influences and fostered a reactionary social and literary aristocracy. Meanwhile numbers of the public at large had access only to the basest products of the scribbler's art and languished in a slough of ignorance. Hence, in the period when English liberty was in process of triumphing over medieval absolutism, nationalism over civil strife and foreign domination, intelligence and intellectual curiosity over superstition,—but for the work of the translators, broad English culture would have been later than it was in arriving.

The exceedingly large number of translations from the classics which were made in the dozen or more years previous to 1572 has been from time to time subject for comment, but no very well-considered reason for their appearance seems ever to have been assigned. Time, moreover, has thrown so much obscurity about many of the phrases in the translators' dedicatory letters and prefaces, that it is difficult to draw inferences concerning the motives that led to this sudden activity. It is now proposed to rediscover, if possible, the meaning of the quite informal and oftentimes allusive statements of these various fugitive compositions just referred to and to weave the suggestions thus obtained and such information as is

edited Heywood's translations of three of Seneca's plays, with introduction and notes (*Jasper Heywood and His Translations*, 1913); Jockers has dealt also with other plays rendered in the period from the same classical author (*Die Englischen Seneca-Uebersetzer des 16 Jahrhundert*, 1909); and E. M. Spearing (*The Elizabethan Translations of Seneca's Tragedies*, 1912; *cf. Modern Language Review*, 1909, pp. 437 ff.) has discussed the entire group of Seneca's tragedies put out in the Elizabethan period. The last named has also edited Studley's *Agamemnon and Medea* (*Studley's Translations*, 1913).

available from other sources into an intelligible account. Should it be objected that dedications and prefaces are generally flattering or conventional, the apparently ingenuous, specific, reiterated, and mutually corroborative statements of the translators must be allowed to speak for themselves. Besides, the position of the early translators differed fundamentally from that of renaissance scholars in general. In publishing a classical book in English, one recommended it for the perusal of others and accordingly acknowledged a certain amount of responsibility for it. It is, therefore, unlikely that the dedications and prefaces were written without serious purpose.

The specific period here covered begins with the last half of Edward's reign (*i.e.*, 1550-1553) and includes the first decade or decade and a half after Elizabeth's accession (1558), the whole of Mary's time being passed over as one of reaction. Within these limits nearly, if not quite, all the influences that caused the interest in the translation of the classics, manifested themselves; and before the close of the period the literature of modern Italy had become a rival for the nation's attention. By 1572 large numbers of the classical writings then best known had made their appearance in English, and the first translators were turning their efforts into other channels. Politically, and culturally also, English history had entered a new phase.

The subjects for study bearing upon this appearance of translations may be briefly analyzed as follows: (1) the degree of popular interest in classical learning previous to Elizabeth's time, and the political, religious, and language conditions that may have led to a translation activity; (2) the discoverable evidence of a self-conscious movement for the translation of the classics into English; (3) the sympathies and interests of the translators, the translators' patrons, and their public; (4) the objects of the "movement," and its relation to the progress of English culture, religion, morals, and politics; (5) opposition to the "movement," the identification of the opponents, and the details of the contest waged between them and the translators; (6) the fate of the "movement."

CHAPTER I

The First Part of the Sixteenth Century

COMPARED with contemporary culture in some other countries, particularly Italy, early English humanism tended to be liberal rather than pedantic, as mere reference to the names of many of the classical scholars from Erasmus to Cheke and Wilson at the end of Henry VIII's reign shows. Moreover, in common with northern peoples in general, Englishmen clung to moral ideals. Elyot, More, Ascham, among others, employed their energies in giving the renaissance in England this turn, and the immoral tone of classical writings was either ignored by them, or else not perceived. For a time also the liberal movement remained non-iconoclastic. Colet, Grocyn, and More brought the lamp of learning from Italy without introducing paganism, irreligiousness, or overt threat to existing institutions. The first humanists were all good sons of the church, seeking only correction of ecclesiastical and moral abuses, not severance from Rome or political upheaval. Erasmus, as Cardinal Gasquet has shown,[1] probably had little direct sympathy with the reformation; More wrote what to some seems a radical political tract, the *Utopia*, as the finest fruit of his classical studies and then accepted the chancellorship in the despotic government of Henry. Because of a belief

[1] *The Eve of the Reformation*, 1905, pp. 152, 169.

in the exclusiveness of learning the English renaissance at its inception was confined to a small group of the *intelligentzia*. Only certain classes, in particular scholars and some of the nobility who were versed in the classical languages, studied the ancients. Even to writers on education, such as Erasmus, author of *The Education of a Christian Prince*, Elyot, of the *Gouernour*, and Vives,[2] of *De Institutione feminae christianae*, the idea of a general dissemination of classical knowledge never occurred.

The Downfall of the Old Learning

SOON, however, political and ecclesiastical events were to be instrumental in making humanism a general issue. Although from an early period the reformation party was fundamentally in accord with the principles of the renaissance, it was not at first generally so considered, and the early attacks upon the institutions of the old learning were indirect and were prompted by ulterior motives. Few persons, if any, foresaw what far-reaching results the fall of the monasteries and, with them, of many of the educational institutions of the country was to have. Scholars in great numbers were deprived of their livings, and the splendid libraries housed by ecclesiastics were scattered. The secondary schools[3] also suffered great injury in Henry's and Edward's reigns, many of them being totally destroyed with no provision for their reëstablishment, so that "not one tithe of those which previously existed"[4] remained.

[2] These three men wrote with the nobility in mind, Vives' special care being the young Princess Mary.

[3] A majority of these were in some way dependent upon ecclesiastical institutions. (Leach, *English Schools at the Reformation, 1546-1548*, pp. 5 ff.; Watson, *English Grammar Schools to 1660*, pp. 15-16.)

[4] *Cambridge History of English Literature*, 1909, 3 : 50; see also Miles Wilson in Strype's *Cranmer*, 2 : 162-163.

At the universities, a quarter of a century of visitations, burning of books, and trials for heresy brought about lamentable conditions. With the destruction of the monastic institutions, an important source of students from among the nobility and gentry as well as from other classes,[5] the numbers taking degrees decreased at both Oxford and Cambridge. "At Oxford in 1535 one hundred and eight men graduated, while, in 1536, only fifty-four did so. Up to the end of Henry's reign, the average was fifty-seven; in Edward's, thirty-three; while during the revival of the old thought under Mary, it rose again as high as seventy. The decrease of students at Cambridge was not at first so formidable. This was natural, since that university was far more in sympathy with the new ideas than was her sister. But ten years after the dissolution a serious decrease showed itself." "Between 1555 and 1559 only one hundred and seventy-five proceeded to the bachelor's standing at Cambridge, and two hundred and sixteen at Oxford, less hostile to the dominant powers. . . . In the last year of Mary, only twenty-eight degrees in arts had been conferred at Oxford."[6]

Although it was under the name of the reformation that all this havoc was wrought to the old learning, humanism with right came to be held co-responsible. As Preserved Smith says,

Luther himself saw, as early as 1523, the connection between his movement and the revival of learning, which he compared to a John the Baptist preparing the way for the preaching of the gospel. . . . Foxe, while maintaining that the overthrow of the

---

[5] Traill, *Social England*, 1895, 3:91-92.

[6] *Cambridge History of English Literature*, 1909, 3:50, 421. For the decline in higher degrees, see Huber, *History of the English Universities* (abridged and edited by F. W. Newman, 1843), 1:291. *Cf.* Traill, *Social England*, 1895, 3:266. *Zurich Letters*, May 22 and June 1, 1560.

papacy was a great miracle and an everlasting mercy, yet recognized that it was rendered possible by the invention of printing and by the "first push and assault" given by the ungodly humanists.[7]

Similarly Anthony à Wood clearly implies that humanists contributed directly to the downfall of the old learning by bringing it into public disrepute. Writing of Mary's reign, he says,

Though the antient Religion was restored, and all things went as formerly, and to the best apprehensions were like to continue so, yet the ill report of learning now current (especially that which was antient and vulgarly received by our Academicians) deterred many from meddling with it.[8]

In other words, the staggering blows aimed at the church fell with nearly equal strength upon established learning. Conversely, a conscious alliance of the renaissance and the reformation forces became inevitable. The failure of Thomas Cromwell, Henry's chancellor, to construct a policy favorable to the renaissance without regard to the reformation[9] shows the change that had taken place since the days of Erasmus. The monarchy also was losing prestige in the struggle.

Progress of the Renaissance

MEANWHILE the new learning had had notable, though not unqualified, success. Before 1540 a second genera-

[7] *Age of the Reformation*, pp. 700-701. Not only had many of the English reformers, such as Cranmer, Ridley, Lever, and Jewel, but also most of the continental leaders of Protestantism, at least in their earlier years, been distinguished humanists—Calvin, Beza, Bullinger, Melanchthon, Oecolampadius, Peter Martyr, Sturm, Cordier, and Ramus.

[8] *History of the University of Oxford*, Volume 2, Part I, p. 135.

So far as possible, the quotations in this study have been made to conform in matters of spelling and punctuation with the corresponding passages in the editions used. The dates appearing in connection with works cited are usually those of publication.

[9] Green, *Short History of the English People*, p. 354.

tion of humanists had appeared, some of whom were
nearly as brilliant as the first. At St. John's, Cambridge,
were studied "with the greatest zeal the choicest authors
of the best period";[10] and similar conditions obtained in
many of the other colleges. The significance, if not the
extent, of the liberal movement may be measured by reference to some of the men who resided at the universities.
At St. John's, Cambridge, were Ascham,[11] author, tutor
of Princess Elizabeth, and diplomat, and Cecil,[12] later
Elizabeth's Prime Minister and chief member of her government. At Queen's was Smith,[13] Cecil's life-long friend,
who became professor of civil law at Cambridge in
1543/4 and served as vice-chancellor. Later he was successively Elizabeth's ambassador to Paris, and Secretary
of State. At King's was Wilson, the future author of the
Arte of Logic, and the *Arte of Rhetorique*, and the translator of Demosthenes (1570), who in 1581 after a score
of years in public service of various sorts succeeded Smith
as Secretary of State. The two Hobys, who performed
important diplomatic missions for later governments (one
of them, Sir Thomas, now best known as the translator

---

[10] Ascham, *Scholemaster* (Arber edition, p. 135).

[11] For brief biographies of writers and translators dealt with in this
volume, see pp. 129-154, *infra*.

[12] Sir William Cecil (1520-1598) was Secretary of State under Somerset, and after a period of retirement during the reign of Mary was the
most conspicuous agent in the placing of Elizabeth upon the throne.
He was Prime Minister from the beginning of her reign till his death,
and became chancellor of Cambridge in 1559. He was created Lord
Burleigh in 1571. In early life he was an enthusiastic humanist. His
first wife was Cheke's sister Anne, and his second, Mildred, the daughter
of the reformer Sir Anthony Cooke. For facts concerning Cheke see
below.

[13] Sir Thomas Smith (1513-1577) was one of the distinguished Cambridge scholars of Henry's reign. He successively received the degrees
of B.A. (1529/30), M.A. (1533), and LL.D. (1542). He was a member
of Somerset's government and a foreign emissary. He early adopted
Protestant views and at one time engaged in protecting reformers from
the hostility of Bishop Gardiner.

of the *Courtier*) were both Cambridge men of this period. Above all, Cheke,[14] the strongest personality among the second generation of English renaissance scholars, was Greek lecturer at the university. Grimald, though he later proved unworthy of the reformers' confidence, for a time was upholding the cause of humanism at Oxford.[15] Many of the nobility outside of the universities also were enthusiastic adherents of the renaissance.

Opposition and Deflection

THOUGH restrained and demoralized, the old thought was by no means dead; instead, it was stirred to antagonism and for a long time continued a militant and, to a marked degree, a dominating influence. For at least two decades after the accession of Elizabeth, Oxford vigorously resisted the inroads of liberalism,[16] and the majority of the nation, which remained Catholic[17] until well into the sixties, naturally clung to their old intellectual leaders. During the revival of the old learning in the time of Mary, Gardiner and likewise, presumably, Pole, the chan-

[14] Sir John Cheke (1514-1557) was noted for an improved method of Greek pronunciation, which he was compelled by the government to discontinue, and for his advocacy of unlatinized English. He was a distinct inspiration to the liberal leaders of the time and rendered a real service to the reformation and the renaissance in England by encouraging scholarship among the exiles at Padua during the reign of Mary. Just previous to his death he was compelled to recant Protestantism, but at once deeply regretted his act.

[15] See p. 138, *infra.*

[16] Wood writes of a Ramian, one John Barebones, who had the option of recanting or being expelled from Oxford in 1574 (*op. cit.*, 1 : II, p. 176); and a fistic encounter between a Ramian and an Aristotelian is referred to by Richard Harvey (*Plaine Percival, Puritan Discipline Tracts*, 1860, p. 30). The work of reforming Oxford probably began about 1564, when Leicester became chancellor; Cecil had been made chancellor of Cambridge in 1559.

[17] Preserved Smith, *op. cit.*, pp. 325-328; Froude, *History of England*, 7 : 11 and note.

cellors of the universities, in spite of their both having been students of the classics, were pronouncedly hostile to the renaissance.[18] At Cambridge, after about 1540, when the enthusiasm for the study of Greek aroused by Cheke and Smith had been quenched by the arbitrary measures of Gardiner, "Greek as a university study steadily declined," while "under Mary, it was reputed to have disappeared from Oxford."[19] Of the latter place, during the time of the Catholic reaction, Wood writes,

The Magistrates now had a greater care to the enriching and well ordering of the University, as also for the establishment of the Catholic Religion than for the retrieving of Learning.[20]

Statutes and injunctions of Henry's and Edward's reigns establishing humanistic studies at the two universities were repealed,[21] these studies being considered in part the cause of apostasy.[22] Moreover, the roll of the Protestant exiles, such as Wilson, Cooke, Jewel, Grindal, Parker, Humphrey, and many others, at Geneva, Frankfort, Strasburg, and elsewhere during the time of Mary, when both Protestantism and the new learning were under the ban, reveals how large a company of enlightened men for the time being had been dispensed with. Cheke and Grimald, the humanistic leaders at Cambridge and Ox-

[18] "To Ascham the arch-enemy of English learning was the catholic restoration. . . . Gardiner was hard on Trinity and St. John's, Cambridge."—*Cambridge History of English Literature*, 1909, 3:410, 420.

[19] *Ibid.*, 3:424; *cf.* 3:52-53.

[20] *Op. cit.*, 2:1:135.

[21] *Cambridge History of English Literature*, 1909, 3:420.

[22] Stokes in addressing Queen Mary's visitors at Cambridge in 1556, upon the abuses of the preceding years, attributed the Protestant symbolical interpretation of the Eucharist to a habit of the renaissance "philosophers," acquired from Epicurus and his followers, of employing the word *quasi* to aid in establishing their positions. Lamb, *A Collection of Letters, Statutes, and other Documents, from MS. Library of Corp. Christ. Coll. illustrative of the History of Cambridge*, p. 179.

ford respectively, were compelled to recant their liberal[23] views; Wilson was trailed to Italy and given over to the Inquisition; Cranmer and Ridley perished in the persecutions.

The diminished number of degrees conferred at the universities after 1535 indicates that interest in the new learning was not sufficiently general to offset the losses attendant upon the decline of the old education. Complaints were often recorded by various writers concerning the indifference of the rising generation of gentry toward study. In 1529 John Palsgrave noted that persons about his pupil, the young Duke of Richmond, natural son of Henry VIII, were making efforts through the diversions of sports and entertainments "to bring his [the Duke's] mind from learning" and "let not to say that learning is a great hindrance to and displeasure to a nobleman."[23a] A similar complaint concerning the indifference of the young nobility appears in the *Scholemaster*. Ascham writes,

Yet I heare saie, some yong Ientlmen of oures count it their shame to be counted learned. . . . A marvelous case, that Ientlemen shold be so ashamed of good learning and never a whit ashamed of ill manners.[24]

A parvenu gentry, sons of the middle class suddenly grown wealthy, sought the universities with no serious purpose, and added to the general demoralization. This

[23] "No one case marks more clearly [than Cheke's] the special point of the Marian persecution—its systematic attack on men of light and leading. It was not the number but the quality of its victims that so stirred Englishmen. Cranmer, Latimer, Hooper, Ridley, Cheke, Philpotts, Ferrar, Bradford, Bland, and Taylor—it was the degrading and burning of such men that recalled, in a more odious shape, the terror of Thomas Cromwell."—Traill, *Social England*, 1895, 3:191.

[23a] *Letters and Papers, Foreign and Domestic, of the Reign of Henry VIII*, 4:5806. *Cf.* Elyot, *Gouernour*, 1:12.

[24] *Op. cit.*, p. 60. *Cf.* Elyot, *op. cit.*, 1:12.

stagnated condition of learning was self-perpetuating, for, as Professor Huber states, the universities produced poor tutors for gentlemen, and they in turn became unpromising students at the universities.[25]

The turning of the more promising youth, chiefly younger sons of the gentry, from liberal studies to a pursuit of law was a further cause for regret on the part of older men like Paynell, for example, who in his *Conspiracie of Catiline* (1541) could not refrain from interpolating into his text the following:

Elas what a time be we in: for nowe a dayes onlye the schole maysters in a maner do giue and lerne vs the preceptes of Eloquence: and euery man for desire of luker and money, gothe in hande to studye the lawe. Whereof it folowethe, that all we be but as baabes, and can not declare and expresse, that we haue conceiued in our myndes.[26]

Because of the superior pecuniary and social advantages of the legal profession, parents and advisers permitted this deflection and sometimes even urged it upon reluctant youths,[27, 28] so that much is heard during the Elizabethan period of the overcrowded condition at the inns of court.[29]

The Period of the Revolution

OF the events in the first part and middle of the sixteenth century, the one of greatest importance to the

[25] *Op. cit.*, 1 : 334.

[26] End of Chapter XIII (quoted from edition of 1557).

[27] Strype, *Annals of the Reformation*, Pt. I, 1 : 538.

[28] See Elyot, *op. cit.*, 1 : 13. John Dolman undertook the study of law "partly by the counsel of them that might comaund me and partlye by mine own consent."—*Tusculanian Discourses*, Dedication.

"For I needes / (no helpe) a whyle go toyle,
In Studies, that / no kynde of muse delyght."
—Googe, *Eglogs, Epytaphes, and Sonettes* (Arber edition, p. 90).

[29] Inderwick, *Records of the Inner Temple*, p. lxxix.

growth of liberalism was the Protestant revolution in Edward's reign. Then the smoldering desires of the nation for political liberty and for intellectual enlightenment were temporarily realized. With the persistence and increase of the liberal spirit fostered and furthered by devotion to the classics, all illusions concerning the reconcilability of the old faith and the renaissance were completely dissipated, and the belief in the exclusiveness of learning was thrown aside by the ruling classes. At the same time, Lutheranism was supplanted by Calvinism, a rationalistic type of theology more closely related to humanism and intellectual freedom. Some of the leading nobles, including the Duke of Northumberland,[30] the head of the state, became active patrons of the new learning; and in general, through the efforts of substantially the same leaders that later put and maintained Elizabeth upon the throne, the cause of popular government, Protestantism, and the renaissance all received great impetus. Simultaneously the translation activity which was to flourish in the Elizabethan period, though presently with the accession of Mary it was destined to be momentarily interrupted, had its beginning.

[30] Wilson, *Arte of Rhetorique,* Dedication (1553). The official encouragement given to the spread of classical and liberal ideas by the government in Edward's reign is recorded in verses introducing Nicolls' translation of Thucydides (1550). The writer speaks of knowledge of antiquity as

> "absenced
> So longe from youe of thys famouse Region.
> Whyche nowe our Kynge, of hys haboundant grace,
> Wyth hys highe Counsailles delyberation,
> Frankely hath graunted to be in euery place
> Good studie to preferre, all slouthe to deface,
> That the goodnes therein beinge vertuously vsed:
> The contraries also may prudently be exchued."

The State of Latin and English

THE language situation in the middle of the century also tended to stimulate interest in the translation of classical writings. With education and educational institutions in such low state, ability to read the classical languages with ease was comparatively rare. In spite of the many efforts to educate children in spoken Latin,[31] the results, to judge from Ascham's remarks, must have been more formal than substantial.

"Speake," he says, "the master careth not, the scholar knoweth not what. . . . The braine should gouerne the tonge, and reason leadeth forth the taulke."[32]

To get learned men for the clergy, Archbishop Parker confessed was impossible.[33] Jewel complained to Peter Martyr that there was a scarcity of preachers and that the schools gave no promise of supply.[34] William Baldwin declared,

And sure it is a shame for all yung men that they be no more studious in the tunges, but the world is now come to that passe, that if hee can prate a little Latin, and handle a Racket and a pair of six square bowles: he shall sooner obtain any liuing then the best learned in a whole Citie, which is the cause that learning is so despised, and bagagicall things so much aduanced.[35, 36]

[31] Watson, op. cit., pp. 315-316.

[32] Op. cit., p. 29. Humanism with its demand that classical Latin be substituted in speech for medieval Latin, did much toward the discontinuance of Latin in conversation. Cf. Berdan, Early Tudor Poetry, pp. 326-328.

[33] Correspondence (Parker Society), August 15, 1560. The great change that had taken place in the matter of language is illustrated by the complaint of Palsgrave twenty years earlier that it was then difficult to get preachers and schoolmasters who could preach and teach competently in English. Acolastus, "Epistle to the Kings Highness."

[34] Zurich Letters, November 6, 1560.

[35] Beware the Cat (1561 ?, 1570). Corser, Collecteana, Anglo-Poetica, 1:111 (Chetham Society, 1860).

[36] Over the state of Greek it is hardly necessary to pause. Interest in the study of it declined seriously after the first part of the century. (Cambridge History of English Literature, 1909, 3: 52-53). Scarcely any

Concomitantly, English was making steady advancement in popularity. The earlier humanists[37] had included the study of the vernacular in the program for the education of the upper classes, and beginning with 1540 English books were used from time to time in the schools.[38] As in all lands, the success of the reformation lay in a direct appeal to the people in their own language. Accordingly, under Henry, the tenets of the new faith had been propagated by means of translations of the Bible and of the Book of Prayer and in the early Elizabethan period by the use of controversial tracts.[39] When the English reformers, returning after the death of Mary,— their ideas of democracy meanwhile having been strengthened by contact with their associates on the Continent,— found the Catholic majority of the nation ignorant of Latin, they began anew to employ the simple vernacular for all purposes. In 1559, despite strong opposition from the reactionaries, the restored Book of Prayer appeared; Archbishop Parker presently issued the *Old Testament;* large audiences listened to preaching in English; and sermons and tracts were published and widely distributed. A great wave of interest in the public singing of religious

books in Greek character were printed in England before Grant's *Graecae Linguae Specilegium* (1575), (Hazlitt, *Schools, School-Books, and School-Masters*, p. 251). According to Woodward (*Cambridge History of English Literature*, 1909, 3:424) no translator "Savile excepted" rendered a Greek author without recourse to a French version. Barker (Palmer, p. 118), Drant (see *Horace*, Preface, 1567), Sanford (*Epictetus*, t.p.), and Wilson (*Demosthenes*) may have constituted further exceptions to this statement.

[37] Elyot, Vives, and latterly Ascham.

[38] Palsgrave, *op. cit.*

[39] Considerable knowledge of these tracts, especially in Elizabeth's reign, is obtainable from notices in Dibdin-Ames, Volume 4. *Cf.* also Parker, *Correspondence* (Parker Society), p. 220, and *Zurich Letters*, August 21, 27, and September 1, 1561.

songs[40] demonstrates the enthusiasm of the people with respect to the new privileges afforded by the use of English in religious matters and also the power that the language was coming to have. The conscious use of English by the reformers for obtaining popular support is further illustrated by the words of Parkhurst written to Bullinger with reference to the republication in English of Foxe's *Martyrs*, formerly issued in Latin.

"Foxe," he says, "has written a large volume on the English Martyrs, and that too in English; it was published four days before Easter. The papists themselves are now beginning to be disgusted with the cruelty of their leaders."[41]

Thus the time was ripe for the general dissemination of the new learning through the vernacular, an important part, as will be shown, of the program of the restored revolutionary party.

[40] *Zurich Letters*, Jewel to Peter Martyr, March 5, 1560.
[41] *Ibid.*, April 26, 1563.

CHAPTER II

A SURVEY OF THE TRANSLATION MOVEMENT

Number of Translations

BEFORE the purposes of what is here for conven-
ience to be called the translation movement are
considered, the existence of such a movement
should be shown.[1] The separate translations which appeared during the first decade of Elizabeth's reign (1558-
1568), exclusive of reprints, considerably exceeded all
that were published in Henry VIII's whole reign, thirty-
nine and thirty-six respectively.[2] In other words, the translating activity increased fourfold, a rate nearly maintained until the end of 1572, when a large proportion of
the most prized classical writings had received English
dress. From then till the last decade of the century, the

[1] The present study has been based throughout upon the translations
cited by Miss Henrietta R. Palmer in her *List of English Editions and
Translations of Greek and Latin Classics Printed before 1641*, prepared
for the Bibliographical Society, 1911; where there has been occasion to
depart from her work note has been made of the fact. For complete
titles of translations the reader is referred to that study.

[2] Douglas' Scottish version of *Vergil* is omitted here and later. *The
Life of Vergil* (one in Henry's and one in Elizabeth's reign), *Guevara*
(one in Henry's reign, and one in Mary's), and supposititious works
(five in Henry's reign), given by Palmer, have been excluded in all
computations, because of their non-classical character. Whithals' *Colu-
mella*, etc. (first ed., 1510, DNB), has been assigned to Henry's reign.
Painter's *Palace of Pleasure* (1566), omitted by Palmer, is counted as
a classical translation, since according to the title page it contains parts
from Herodotus, Aelian, Plutarch, Aulus Gellius, Livy, Tacitus, and
Quintus Curtius. Fulwood's *Enemie of Idlenesse*, which contains translations of parts of Cicero's *Letters* (DNB), has also been included, but
Evans' *Horace* has been omitted owing to doubt concerning its publication.

activity was but two-thirds as great. While in Edward's disturbed reign, translations had appeared sporadically —seven in 1550 and four in 1553, eleven in all[3]—during the Catholic reaction translating had been practically suspended, for of the four translations then published, three appeared in the days of Mary's decline (1557-1558)[4] and hence are properly to be considered the first fruit of the Elizabethan period. In other words, the years 1558-1572 were distinctly the most prolific in printed translations from the classics of any time during the century.[5]

Besides these, several translations which appeared later, or which were never published, were begun in the first years of this reign. In the early sixties Hall was engaged upon his *Homer*;[6] Golding, famed for his translation of the *Metamorphoses*, seems, from remarks of his which appear in the dedication of his translation of Calvin's *Psalms* (1571), to have been contemplating, if he was not already engaged upon, his *Mela Pomponius*

[3] In view of the political and social conditions, a really remarkable showing, and one which discloses the relationship of the translating activity of that period to that of the Elizabethan. Certainly some of the translations belonging to the year 1553 appeared after Mary became queen but have been regarded as due to the interest of the previous reign.

[4] Richard Sherry's *A Treatise of the Figures of Grammer and Rhetorike*, 1555, contains the remaining translation. "The oration which Cicero made to Cesar of Marcus Marcellus."

[5] Translations of Henry's and Edward's reigns reprinted in the years 1558-1572 are the following: Cope's *Livy*, 1543, 1548, 1561, 1568, 1590; Burrant's *Cato*, 1545, 1553, 1560, 1562, n.d.; Harington's *Booke of Freendeship* (Cicero), 1550, 1562; Grimald's *Cicero* ("Duties"), 1553, 1556, 1558, 1568, 1575, 1583, 1596, 1600(?); Brend's *Curtius*, 1553, 1561, 1570, 1584, 1592, 1602, 1614; Bank's *Cato* (Latin and English), 1540, 1553, 1553, 1553, 1555, 1562, 1580, 1592, 1620; Poyntz' *Table of Cebes*, 1535, 1537, 1539, 1560(?). Barclay's *Warre agaynst Iugurth*, 1520(?), reappeared in 1557 with Paynell's *Conspiracie of Catiline* (1544, 1557): The last named is from Felicius based upon Sallust and others; accordingly it is not given by Palmer.

[6] Dedication (1581).

(1587) or his *Solinus* (1587). Googe, the translator of
Palingenius, and Turberville have recorded futile attempts to turn Lucan into English.[7] Googe also began
Aratus.[8] Drant, generally known as the translator of
Horace, completed five books of the *Iliad*,[9] and Brend,
the translator of Quintus Curtius, was engaged upon
Caesar's *Commentaries* when he died.[10] Two contributors
to the *Mirror for Magistrates*, Chaloner and Blenerhasset, the latter while a student at Cambridge, translated
Epistolae Heroidum (Epistle 17)[11] and *Remedio Amoris*[12] respectively; and a part of Vergil by Grimald seems
to be referred to by Googe in his *Epytaphe of Maister
Thomas Phayre*.[13, 14] Hoby[15] and Googe[16] both refer to
others who had begun to translate works which they
themselves published, the one the *Courtier* and the other
the *Zodiake of Lyfe*. While not ancient classics, these
books were of interest to the supporters of the renaissance.

Such a sudden change in the number of translated
books is evidence of a new interest in the classics at the
accession of Elizabeth. But a change, too, in the character

[7] Turberville, *Book of Faulconrie*, Dedication (1575). Rollins dates
this attempt 1571 or before (*Modern Philology*, 15: 527-528). Googe's
attempt is recorded in *Zodiake of Lyfe*, Preface, 1560 (Arber edition of
Eglogs, p. 7).

[8] *Ibid.*

[9] DNB, article, "Drant." On this translator's *Archias*, see p. 146, *infra*.

[10] Golding, *Caesar*, Dedication.

[11] DNB. Printed in Park's *Antiquae Nugae* (1871), 2: 372-389. Of
course, there is no way of knowing that Chaloner's work was not done
considerably before Elizabeth's reign, but in that case he would have
to be credited with being the first translator of Ovid.

[12] DNB.

[13] Googe, *Eglogs, Epytaphes, and Sonettes* (Arber edition, pp. 73-74).

[14] Churchyard did portions of Vergil and Pliny, but these probably
belong to a later period. DNB. Queen Elizabeth translated a letter of
Seneca for John Harington, 1567 (Park, *op. cit.*, 1: 109-114).

[15] *Courtier*, Dedication.

[16] *Zodiake of Lyfe*, Dedication, 1565 (Arber edition of the *Eglogs*,
p. 13).

of the works translated occurred. In Henry's reign most of the translations from classical authors fall under the headings of school-books and scientific or philosophical works. Of the whole thirty-six translations appearing in about as many years, only four or five were histories;[17] three of the five translations of Cicero were by the same hand;[18] Cato appeared only once; and except for the *Andria* (1520?) of Terence and Surrey's fourth book of Vergil's *Aeneid* (1548) there was no poetry.[19] That is to say, up to the year 1557 (with some allowance for Edward's reign) classical history, Cicero's works, poetry, and romance—so far at least as published translations indicate—had received little or no attention. Of the eleven translations of Edward's reign—the period of the short-lived beginnings of new national life and of relatively increased activity in translation—four histories, three parts of Cicero, and one book of cosmography appeared; and with the coming of Elizabeth, works of history, liberal philosophy, poetry, and romance became more numerous. Nineteen of the thirty-nine translations belonging to the first decade of the reign were poetry, seven were history, and one was romance.[20] If Underdown's *Heliodorus*, which appeared early in 1569, be included, the number of the romances would have to be increased to two.[21] Of the translations never published

---

[17] Barclay's *Warre agaynst Iugurth* (Sallust) (1520?); Rastell's *Caesar* (1530?); Paynell's *Conspiracie of Catiline* (Felicius, dependent upon Sallust and others) (1541); Cope's *Livy* (1544). Under some classifications Morison's *Frontinus* (1539) might be included under the heading of histories.

[18] Whittington, *De Officiis* (1520); *Cato Maior* (1530); *Paradox* (1540).

[19] *Flowers for Latin Speaking* from Terence by Udall (1533) is here classified as a schoolbook.

[20] See pp. 129-134, *infra*.

[21] For reasons already stated the translations published in 1557 and

or published later (cited above), nine were poetry, two history, and one cosmography.

This change of interest may be illustrated in still another way. The free cultural spirit of the ancients appears to have taken effect slowly in the first part of the sixteenth century, and the aims of the first translators of histories seem to have been somewhat narrow. But at the time of the revolution a broader spirit entered the translators, for the histories belonging to the years 1550 and 1553—Nicolls' *Thucydides*, Smyth's *Herodian*, Brend's *Quintus Curtius*, and Paynell's *Dares*, as is shown in their dedications—represent the beginnings of a cultural interest, and the dedication of the first three of them respectively, to Sir John Cheke, the liberal Cambridge scholar, to Sir William Herbert, the Earl of Pembroke, of Calvinistic views, and to John Dudley, the Duke of Northumberland, a patron of the new learning, evidence an affiliation of the translators with the liberals in government and religion. The three translations of Cicero in Edward's time—Harington's *Booke of Freendeship* (1550), Grimald's *Duties* (1553) and Wilson's *Arte of Rhetorique* (1553)[22] also manifest an enlarged outlook.[23] At the end of Mary's reign, upon the resumption of the publication of translations, commencing with Surrey's and Phaer's renderings of the *Aeneid* and Bury's *Isocrates*, the liberal spirit became a national force both in thought and politics.

1558, two of Vergil and one each of Isocrates and Cato (both of the last-named in the same volume) might be added to the Elizabethan accomplishment.

[22] Contains the *Rhetorica*. Palmer fails to note Wilson's indebtedness to Quintilian and Aristotle (see Mair edition, pp. xix-xx).

[23] All three of these men, just mentioned, suffered for the Protestant cause. Katherine, Duchess of Suffolk, Harington's patron, was mother of two young "Dukes of Suffolk," and stepmother of Lady Jane Grey.

• *The Personnel of the Movement*

THAT more than a coterie was interested in the instilling of classical ideals into the minds of the general public need not be left to mere conjecture, for in the preface to the translation of Seneca's *Thyestes* (1560) Heywood has furnished very definite clues as to the existence of a compact, self-conscious, renaissance movement. Arber's comment, on the basis of this passage, that translation was a "rage"[24] is quite inadequate. Heywood names eight, and hints at many more, young enthusiastic translators and writers gathered together at the inns of court—places already associated with several of the earliest translators of the classics—and moreover he suggests the existence of a feeling of antipathy between them and the recognized scholars of the realm.[25] Because of its importance, a part of Heywood's description is here given.

But yf thy will be rather bent, / a yong mans witt to proue,
And thinkst that elder lerned men / perhaps it shall behoue,
Jn woorks of waight to spende theyr tyme, / goe where Mineruaes men,
And finest witts doe swarme :[(a)] whome she / hath taught to passe with pen.
Jn Lyncolnes Jnne and Temples twayne, / Grayes Jnne and other mo,
Thou shalt them fynde whose paynfull pen / thy verse shall florishe so,

[24] Googe, *Eglogs* (Arber edition, p. 5). Ward's characterization of the translation activity as "the choicest kind of literary productivity" likewise falls short of the mark (*English Dramatic Literature*, 1 : 188).

[25] *Cf.* Hoby, quoted pp. 102-103, *infra.*

"The thirde and last reason [for making his translation] was, that they of riper yeares and exacter knowlege shoulde be pricked (as it wer with a spurre) by thys my doing, to the attemptyng of some worke to remain for an attestation that they liued not brutishely, but as men regarding their vocation."—Watson, *Polybius*, "To the Reader." See also pp. 88-90, *infra.*

[(a)] *Cf.* Googe, *Zodiake of Lyfe*, 1561 (Arber edition of *Eglogs*, p. 8, ll. 1-6).

That Melpomen thou wouldst well weene / had taught them for
    to wright,
And all their woorks with stately style, / and goodly grace
    t'endight.
There shalt thou se the selfe same Northe, / whose woorke his
    witte displayes,
And Dyall dothe of Princes paynte, / and preache abroade his
    prayse.
There Sackuyldes Sonetts sweetely sauste / and featly fyned bee,
There Nortons ditties do delight, / there Yeluertons doo flee
Well pewrde with pen; such yong men three, / as weene thou
    mightst agayne,
To be begotte as Pallas was, / of myghtie Joue his brayne.
There heare thou shalt a great reporte, / of Baldwyns worthie
    name,
Whose Myrrour dothe of Magistrates, / proclayme eternall fame.
And there the gentle Blunduille is / by name and eke by kynde,
Of whome we learne by Plutarches lore, / what frute by Foes to
    fynde,
There Bauande bydes, that turnde his toyle / a Common welthe
    to frame,
And greater grace in Englyshe geues, / to woorthy authors name.
There Googe a gratefull gaynes hath gotte, / reporte that run-
    neth ryfe,
Who crooked Compasse dothe describe, / and Zodiake of lyfe.
And yet great nombre more, whose names / yf J shoulde now
    resight,
A ten tymes greater woorke then thine, / J should be forste to
    wright.
A pryncely place in Parnasse hill, / for these there is preparde,
Where crowne of glittryng glorie hangs, / for them a ryght re-
    warde.[26]

Nowhere else might new ideas have been so likely to
take root and flourish as at the inns of court.[26a] Member-

---

[26] Heywood, *Thyestes*, Preface, ll. 251-302.

[26a] The translation movement had little, if any, connection with the
schools, and there were few schoolmasters among the translators. See p.
27 n. There are, however, instances on record of English versions of
Latin books intended for schoolroom use. Palsgrave in 1549 translated his
Acolastus for this purpose, but his example was probably not often followed. For a while in Elizabeth's time classics in parallel Latin and
English versions known as "constructions" appeared; such, for example,

ship in these institutions was the means taken by the gentry[27] to secure a foothold in the society of the capital. "Here they entered," as Hume says in his biography of Cecil, "to give them some definite standing or pursuit in London, rather than with a view of their becoming practising lawyers."[28] Though the inns were the law schools of the nation, they were communities with living quarters and dining halls, where membership was for life and close relations existed between the "benchers" and the "apprentices."[29] These places were the resort of the great men of the realm. For example, at the frequent banquetings and entertainments "the Queen's Councillors and other very honourable persons"[30] were present. The Earl of Leicester and the Lord Keeper of the Great Seal, Sir Nicholas Bacon, were members of the Inner Temple, the former in particular appearing to have been an interested and active patron.[31] Cecil seems also to have continued to have an active interest in Gray's Inn, where a large proportion of the translators' noble patrons resorted.[32] From early times the inns had been places of social life and liberal culture.[33] The long intervals between mootings and readings, as well as the community life pursued, gave ample

as T. W.'s selections from Cicero's letters (1575); the *Epistle of Cicero* (anonymous, 1589); Fleming's *Eclogues* (1575) and *Bucolics* of Vergil (1589). The employment of the word "students" by Nicolls, Phaer, Heywood, and Studley to designate some of those for whose benefit their work was intended is ambiguous, though Phaer specifically says that his book is not a "construction."

[27] "For that the younger sort are either gentlemen, or sons of gentlemen, or of other most wealthy persons." Stowe in Herbert's *Antiquities of the Inns of Court and Chancery*, p. 173.

[28] *The Great Lord Burghley*, p. 11. *Cf.* Bellot, *Inner and Middle Temple*, p. 127.

[29] Jenks, *A Short History of English Law*, p. 202.

[30] Inderwick, *Inner Temple, Its Early History as Illustrated by its Records*, p. lxv.

[31] See pp. 26, 41, *infra*.

[32] See pp. 39-40, *infra*.   [33] Inderwick, *op. cit.*, lxxix.

opportunity and stimulus for literary pursuits, and such occasions as the great pageant held in Leicester's honor[34] at the Inner Temple during the Christmas season of 1561 must have had an immensely stimulating effect upon literary as well as dramatic interest.[35] Moreover, the nature and the traditions of these institutions were favorable to a spirit of non-compliance. In the thirteenth century the inns had been forward in the revolt against Romanism; and common law, studied at the inns of court, was fundamentally at variance with canon and civil law, studied at the universities.[36] This early liberal spirit continued to be unmolested, for lawyers and law students by their very occupation enjoyed immunity from persecution. In the eighties, for example, the Templars for a time succeeded in retaining Walter Travers, the Puritan, at the Temple church, although Thomas Hooker, the Anglican, was the authorized lecturer. This was "in effect to retain half the Lawyers in England to be of Councell against the ecclesiastical government thereof."[37]

Of the fifty-four known translators of the classics[37a] working between the years 1558 and 1572, inclusive, twenty-three or twenty-five[38] were actually members of

[34] Leicester was the chief performer in the pageant, of which Arthur Broke is thought to have been the author. Inderwick, *op. cit.*, pp. lxiv, lxvi, 220.

[35] On the attention given to the drama at the inns, see *ibid.*, lxix-lxii. *Gorboduc*, written by Sackville and Norton, was performed at the Inner Temple on Twelfth Night, 1561.

[36] Jenks, *op. cit.*, p. 202.

[37] Fuller, *Church History of Britain*, Bk. IX, p. 218.

[37a] There were nine anonymous translations published during these years.

[38] Phaer, Blundeville, Heywood, Barker, Googe, Norton, Dolman, Hall, Neville, Hill, Whitehorne, Haward, Brend, Fulwood, White, Peend, Studley, Chaloner, Turberville, Hubbard, Newton(?), Sadler, Gascoigne, Kenwelmersh, and perhaps Underdown. See pp. 129-134, *infra*.

the inns of court and certainly two, possibly four, others,[39] had some status there, to say nothing of five[40] about whom there is little or no information. Three[41] other members produced their classical translations too late to be counted among the first fifty-four, and four[42] had been pre-Elizabethan translators. Three translators[43] of renaissance authors and eight writers,[44] three of whose names appear in Heywood's list of "Minerva's men," were also enrolled. Two translators[45] of renaissance writers, one of them Hoby—an able defender of the translation of the ancients—and one translator of the classics,[46] were government officials, and as such certainly had many friends at the inns.[47] Still another[48] translator of a classical author was a wealthy London merchant, who later became Lord Mayor. Consequently, though the liberal and popular renaissance movement originated at Cambridge in the reigns of Henry and Edward, the majority of its supporters in the reign of Elizabeth were to be found at the inns of court working together for the spread of new ideas.

[39] Golding, Watson, and probably Churchyard. See pp. 132, 134, and p. 148, *infra*. The fact that Twyne like Watson chose a lawyer for patron suggests their connection with the inns of court.

[40] Howell, Alday, Adlington, Stocker, Candish, Blenerhasset.

[41] Baker, Roll, and North. The last-named appears on Heywood's list (p. 24, *supra*) as the translator of the pseudo-classical work of Guevara. See p. 18, note 2, *supra*.

[42] Nicolls, Paynell, W. Rastell, Salisbury.

[43] Bavand, Broke, Beverley.

[44] Ascham, Baldwin, Ferrers, Sackville, Hake, Parker, Yelverton, Cavyll.

[45] Hoby, Fenton.

[46] Wilson.

[47] The remaining translators of the classics in the early part of Elizabeth's reign fall into two groups: clergymen—Nuce, Turner, Drant, Gilby(?), and possibly Underdown; schoolmen—Evans, Sanford, Grant, Grimald.

[48] Billingsley.

Characteristics of the Movement

OTHER procurable data[49] reveal further evidence of the homogeneous character of the translation movement. It was essentially non-scholarly. Several of the fifty-four, among them some of the most important of the translators, did not attend Oxford or Cambridge; and a large proportion of the rest had stayed for but part of their course, had not yet graduated, or were but recent graduates, when their translations were made.[50] This avoidance or desertion of the universities by some may have been due in a measure to the religious disturbances of the times. For example, Golding, one of the most prominent of the translators, and a Puritan, who entered Jesus College, Cambridge, in 1552, after a single term withdrew on the eve of the Marian restoration. Googe, also a pronounced Protestant, and Turberville, a very outspoken individual, stayed but a short time at Oxford, and very early in Elizabeth's reign were at the inns of court, neither of them having a degree. Yet mere speculation apart, the general conditions at the universities and the cause earlier assigned by Paynell[51] and others for migrations from them account sufficiently for the early departure of many of the most energetic, ambitious young men.

Religiously, the translators, almost without exception,

[49] See pp. 129-134, infra.

[50] Venn and Venn record the entrance but not the graduation of Nicolls (1544), Norton (1544), Hoby (1545), Golding (1552), Billingsley (1567). Whitehorne (1567) can hardly be our translator.—Matriculations and Degrees, Cambridge. Besides these, Blundeville is thought to have been at Cambridge. Phaer only in his very mature age became M.B. and M.D. at Oxford (1559 and 1560). Googe is thought also to have attended Cambridge. A few of the translations may actually have been performed at the universities, for Heywood and Adlington (Oxford) and Studley (Cambridge) signify their university connections on their title pages. Blenerhasset and Grant made their translations at Cambridge. See also under Neville, p. 143, infra.

[51] See p. 13, supra.

were Protestants.[52] Heywood, almost the only Catholic, significantly enough presently eliminated himself. Bound by personal affection to Elizabeth, he at first supported the new régime. But as the trend of events became apparent, he threw his lot in with the other side, leaving England and entering the Society of Jesus at Rome in 1562. The Protestantism of Phaer and Turberville has been called into question,[53] but the former's close friendship for George Ferrers, a prominent opponent of the Roman church, and the latter's for Barnabe Googe should cast doubt upon their ardency for Romanism. On the other hand, Studley, a future follower of Cartwright, Norton, translator of Calvin's *Institutes*, Blundeville, Golding, Gascoigne, Googe, Neville, Drant, Fenton, and Stocker after the first decade or so turned their attention to the promulgation of Puritanism, most of them by translating works of the continental reformers, notwithstanding the growing hostility to the Puritan cause.

The prevailing youth of the translators is also conspicuous. Rarely do the dates of their birth fall before 1535 or 1540, and many of the men did not die till near the end of the century or later. Neville was sixteen when he translated Seneca's *Oedipus;* Studley nineteen when he did the *Agamemnon* and the *Medea;* Googe less than twenty when he published the first edition of *Palingenius;* and Watson "yet in my nonage" when he translated Polybius. Turberville, Fenton, and Hall were under twenty,[53a] and Golding, Heywood, North, and Norton

[52] See pp. 129-134, *infra.*

[53] DNB Article, "Phaer" and *Modern Philology*, 15:527.

[53a] Gascoigne should now be added to this group. Ward and Ambrose, working independently, have fixed upon January, 1541/2, as the date of the poet's birth and November, 1578, as that of his death. The results of their investigations have been recently published in *Review of English Studies*, 2:5:32 ff.; 6:163-172.

under twenty-five at the beginning of the reign; and several like Peend, Nuce, Haward, Hubbard, Newton, Blenerhasset, and others almost certainly belonged to the younger generation. In the cases of Dolman,[54] Googe,[55] Heywood,[56] Howell,[57] Norton,[58] Golding,[59] North[60] Studley,[61] Broke,[62] and Watson[63] special emphasis is given in their own writings, or in the writings of their friends, to the fact of their youth; whereas Heywood and Nuce speak of the youth of the translators as a group.[64] These facts require special consideration.

Of former translators, Barclay, Cope, John Rastell, and Surrey were dead; William Rastell and Nicolls had become barristers of eminence. Phaer, Paynell, and Brend, though still surviving, did not accomplish much more than they had already done. Several of the renaissance scholars, like Cheke, Cranmer, and Ridley, had also died; Ascham was bent with care and disease; Thomas Watson was in the Tower; Cooper, the author of the *Thesaurus Linguae Romanae Britannicae*, and possibly Carre, formerly lecturer in Greek at Cambridge, in order to weather the persecutions of Mary's reign, had been

[54] *Op. cit.*, Preface.

[55] *Zodiake of Lyfe*, 1560. Preface, l. 25 (Arber edition of *Eglogs*, p. 7).

[56] *Thyestes*, Preface.

[57] *Narcissus* (Corser, *Collecteana Anglo-Poetica*, 9 : 104).

[58] *Thyestes*, Preface, l. 275.

[59] Golding refers to his own youth parenthetically, to be sure, but without apology, to account for his ignorance of military matters. *Caesar*, Dedication, 1565. He was thirty years old.

[60] *Diall of Princes*, Dedication.

[61] See complimentary verses prefixed to Studley's *Agamemnon* and *Medea* (Spearing edition, p. 3, l. 126).

[62] Turberville, *Epitaphes, Epigrams, Songes and Sonets*, 1567. "Epitaph on the death of Maister Arthur Broke" (Chalmers, *English Poets*, 2 : 651).

[63] *Polybius*. "To the Reader."

[64] See p. 23 n., *supra*, and p. 35, *infra*.

compelled to turn to medicine.[65] Most important of all,
the fine set of classical students formerly at St. John's
and other Cambridge colleges were occupied with the
work of reconstruction: Parker, Grindal, Jewel, Lever,
Haddon, in the church: Cecil, Wilson, Smith, Cooke, in
the service of the state either at home or abroad.

This should not, however, be taken to indicate that the
work of translation had fallen to young men merely by
default, for youth was regarded by the group at the inns
of court as a special qualification of a translator, Plato
and Cicero being the authorities for this belief. Dolman,
the first one in Elizabeth's reign to render the latter author into English, defends his own youthfulness in the
following terms:

First as for mine owne vnablenes for yeares, I aunswere, by
Plato and this mine authour [Cicero]: that I knowe nothinge,
but that, whiche my soule nowe setled in my body recounteth as
thinges learned before. And the soule, that neuer haue the body
more apte, to whatsoeuer thinge it listeth to to dispose him, then
in his youthe; whyche is, in maner, the greenenesse of the same.
Since therfore, the bodye, whych hath no knowledge, but by reason of the soule, is in youth most apte and able to execute the
inuentions of the same: what cause is there whye the wit, beinge
one of the principall partes of the soule should not chiefelye in
this nimblenes of the bodye, vtter her force and vertue.[66]

This passage when joined with other frequent references
to the translators' youth begins to assume added significance. For example, in lines almost immediately preceding those in which a rivalry between "Minerva's disci-
ples" and "elder men" (quoted above) is suggested,
Heywood, then twenty-five years old, declares,

[65] DNB. Cooper later became Bishop of Winchester, and the inquisi-
tor of the Puritans.

[66] *Op. cit.*, Preface. For a similar remark concerning Studley, see Nuce
in Spearing, *Studley's Translations*, p. 4, ll. 45-46.

> Thou seest dame Nature yet hath sette
> No heares vppon my chinne.[67]

This is a truly astonishing manner of emphasizing the fact of his youth, to which already he has referred six times in the foregoing seventy lines and to which he subsequently continues to refer in the same preface. To these two passages may be added verses of other friends of the translation movement, such as the following, crude as they are,

Grudge not though yonger yeares doe toyle / where horye heddes might wade.
Whose sappye wytte more apter seemes / to trauell in thys trade.
For who can more Mineruas face / then lustye youth expresse ?[68]

or the following,

> Non potes istius calami corrumpere fructus;
> Conseruat famulos magna Minerua suos . . .
> Zoile tuq: furis, iuuenis quum musa triumphet,
> Iratus turges: verbula vana vomis.[69]

All of these citations tend to the conclusion that the young men at the inns of court considered themselves at variance with the established scholars, against whom they had engaged in a contest of considerable bitterness with a feeling of assurance of final victory for their side.

[67] Preface, ll. 245-246.
[68] W. P., verses prefixed to Studley's *Medea* (Spearing edition, p. 126).

Cf. "For though the worke of grauer age, / the connyng seme to craue,
Sumtyme we se yet younger yeares, / a ryper witt to haue.
Accept it therefore, as it is, / (of grener yeres in deede)."—H. C., verses prefixed to Studley's *Agamemnon* (Spearing edition, p. 12).

"*Debuit exemplum quosuis terrere superbos:*
Et, cuius, opus hoc iuuenis, laudare molestum."—Nuce, *ibid.*, p. 3.

"For oft the churlyshe curyous hedd
Condemneth youth as wantyng skyll."—W. R., *ibid.*, p. 11.

[69] *Ibid.*, p. 11.

If such be the case, it would seem that the old hostile alignment that had taken place at the universities early in the century between the new and the old learning was being continued between those of the nation who sought now to disseminate the principles of the renaissance, Protestantism, and nationalism, on the one hand, and the believers in tradition and exclusiveness, represented by the university scholars, Catholic sympathizers, and supporters of the Spanish alliance, on the other.

CHAPTER III

THE POLITICAL ASPECTS OF THE TRANSLATION MOVEMENT

THE prevailing youth of the translators and the emphasis put upon this fact mark the translation movement as a "youth" movement in the modern sense of the term, and in the light of a contemporary statement suggest that it had a political character. Count Feria, the Spanish ambassador, wrote to Philip at the time of Elizabeth's accession,

The kingdom is entirely in the hands of young folks, heretics and traitors, and the Queen does not favour a single man . . . who served her sister. . . . The old people and the Catholics are dissatisfied, but dare not open their lips.[1]

In view of the intimate relations of the renaissance, Protestantism, and the new political régime, is it not possible that after the period of Spanish domination under Philip and Mary, ending with the loss of Calais, the new nobility, who had brought about the revolution in Edward's and Elizabeth's reigns, and the translators, both groups advocating much the same radical political, religious, and philosophical principles, had combined, with "youth" as a slogan, for the improvement and enlightenment of the nation? This theory seems plausible from several considerations.

[1] *Calendar of Letters and State Papers in the Archives of Simancas* (Hume), p. 7.

The Translators' Patriotism

FIRST, the frequent self-dedication of the translators to the service of their country is noteworthy. Heywood, former page of the Princess Elizabeth, now the Queen, declared,

J thought it not repugnāt to my duty if J shold also for a time set a side yᵉ bokes of old Philosophers, Aristotle and Plato, and once endeuour to shew my selfe so louing to my countreye, as to help for the small talēt that god hath geuē me, to conduct by som meanes to further vnderstādīg the vnripened schollers of this realm.[2]

Studley, a former neighbor and an ardent admirer of Cecil, the Prime Minister, said that he produced his translation of Seneca "at the ernest requeste of certaine my familiar frendes," who

willed me, not to hyde & kepe to my selfe that small talent which god hath lente vnto me to serue my countrey wᵗ all, but rather to applye it to the vse of suche yonge Studentes as therby myght take some cōmoditie.[3]

Nuce, still another translator of Seneca, and one of the group who joined in the support and defense of Studley's *Agamemnon* with commendatory and polemical verses, bespeaks in his own translation of *Octavia*, published almost contemporaneously with Studley's work, the patriotism of all the translators.

If [he pleads] the translating of Latine, or other Bookes of other languages, into our mother tong, doth eyther profite the cōmon wealth, or the wryter at all, do not then condemne the yong sprong writers, if that in all pointes they please not thee which may by the grace of God, through thy gētle and curteous accepting of a

---

[2] *Hercules Furens*, Dedication (de Vocht edition, p. 200).

[3] *Agamemnon*, Preface (Spearing edition, p. 23). Googe also published his *Eglogs* at the earnest solicitation of friends. Dedication. (Arber edition, p. 24). See also pp. 37-38, *infra*.

little toye, hereafter employ their labour to more serious and weyghty matters, both to their owne commoditie and thy learning, and especially to the profit of our natiue countrie.[4]

Dolman, a future barrister, translated Cicero in the hope

that our coūtrey, might at length flowe with the workes of philosophye.[5]

Phaer, one who was on intimate terms with the Marquis of Winchester, the Lord Treasurer, stated as his purpose in producing the *Aeneid* in English, the "defence of my countrey language."[6] Golding, a resident at Cecil's house[7] and one in whose translations Cecil took a personal interest,[8] besides fervently voicing to Leicester in the dedication of the *Metamorphoses* his purpose to improve the quality of English culture,[9] and repeatedly instructing his nephew and ward, the young Earl of Oxford,

to procede in learning and vertue (which are thonly ornamentes of nobilitie, or rather the very true nobilitie itself) ī such sort as you may be able to doe acceptable seruice to your Prince and your countrie,[10]

translated *Trogus*, as he tells his reader,

for the zeale I beare to this my natiue countrie, desyrous to gratifie yea and to profite such as haue not vnderstandinge in the Latin tong.[11]

---

[4] "To the Reader."
[5] *Op. cit.*, Dedication.
[6] *Aeneid*, "To the Reader."
[7] See p. 144, *infra*.
[8] See p. 42, *infra*.
[9] *Cf.* p. 68, *infra*.
[10] *Trogus*, Dedication. See also, *Psalms*, Dedication.
[11] *Trogus*, "To the Reader." "The seconde [reason for translating] was a feruent zeale whiche I beare my natiue countrey." Watson, *Polybius*, "To the Reader."

Cf. "If thou art in the way of honour & by reading and practising the liues of the auncients thou hast become a great staffe to the state. . . ." —Lodge, *Catharos*, 1591, fol. 30b.

Bavand, a member of the Middle Temple, one who though not a translator of the classics is placed by Heywood among the men of the new movement, even more specifically voices a political purpose for making his translation:

It behoueth your grace [Elizabeth, to whom the work is dedicated] to be vigilaunt and carefull, that the weightie administration thereof, bee by your good gouuernemente, throughlie executed and discharged, Whiche then cometh to passe, when God is in his creatures trulie glorified and honoured, and the people trained vp in godlie learning, decēt order, and vertuous conversacion. . . . And that your highnesse subiectes of this your common weale of Englande, might the easelier vnderstande the same, for their better instruction, I haue published vnder your graces protection, this peece of worke in our vulgare English toūge, wherin (as nere as I could) I haue doen the dutie of a faiethfull interpretour.[12, 13]

Encouragement by the Nobility

ON the other side, there are many indications that the influential nobility, and especially the members of the government were active in encouraging the translators. Early in the century the old Duke of Norfolk, at a time when chance had ranged him against Wolsey, had urged Barclay to translate the *Warre agaynst Iugurth* (1520?); Wilson's *Arte of Rhetorique* (1553) had been done at

[12] Ferrarius Montanus, *The Good Ordering of a Common Weale*, Dedication.

[13] Neville, Googe, Haward, members of the Inns, Hoby and Wilson, government agents, and in his *Machiavelli* Whitehorne, a soldier, also express patriotic motives for translating. Wilson, who characterizes Demosthenes as "so Necessarie a writer for all those that loue their Countries libertie" (Dedication), says, "He that desires to serue hys Countrie abrode, let hym reade Demosthenes day and nyght, for this is he that is able to make hym fitte to doe any seruice for his Countryes welfare." Preface.

A sense of duty to translate the classics was indigenous not only to England but to every country where the spirit of nationality was rising. See Traill, *Social England*, 1895, 3:347.

the behest of the Duke of Northumberland, then head of the government; the third book of Hoby's *Courtier* was translated in 1551 at the desire of the Marchioness of Northampton,[14] a lady intimate with Lady Jane Grey and the wife of a close associate of the Duke of Northumberland, later a member of Elizabeth's Privy Council; Bury's *Isocrates* (1557) was performed at the desire of his uncle, Sir William Chester, Lord Mayor in 1560; and Golding's *Trogus* was executed in fulfilment of a promise made to his brother-in-law, the elder Earl of Oxford, hereditary great chamberlain; Underdown translated Ovid's *Ibis* (1569) at the request of Lord Buckhurst; and Sadler, *Vegetius* (1572) at the request of Sir Edmund Blundell.[15] Besides, Heywood, Neville, and Hoby, like Studley,[16] were urged to do their work by friends to whom they could "not well deny any thyng y^t frendshyps ryght may seeme iustly to requyre."[17] Finally, Cecil was directly responsible for Golding's translating Caesar and for Wilson's translating Demosthenes; and the circumstances of his intervention, which are described below, suggest the character of the nobility's interest.

An examination of the persons chosen by the translators as patrons shows further how closely in touch with the translation movement the ruling Elizabethan nobles really were. Had the translation of the classics been mere literary exercise,[18] the dedications would probably have been addressed to scattered individuals of more or less prestige, but the following table of dedications of translations and other books put out by the translators during

---

[14] Heading of Book III.
[15] Title pages and dedications.
[16] See p. 35, *supra*.
[17] Neville, *Oedipus*, Dedication.
[18] See p. 23 n., *supra*.

the first fifteen years of Elizabeth's reign shows the patrons chosen to have been almost exclusively influential
members of the court.[19]

* Queen Elizabeth	9
a* Sir William Cecil, Prime Minister (G. I.[20] adm. 1540)	8
a* Sir Nicholas Bacon, Keeper of the Great Seal (G. I. adm. 1532)	1
a* Ladies Cecil and Bacon	1
a* Robert Dudley, Earl of Leicester (I. T.)	8
a* Ambrose Dudley, Earl of Warwick (brother of above)	2
a* Lord Francis Russell, Earl of Bedford (G. I. adm. 1557)	3
a* Countess of Warwick (née Anne Russell) dau. of above	2
a Lord Henry Hastings, Earl of Huntingdon, brother-in-law to the Dudleys (M. T. adm. 1562)	1
a* Lord Thomas Howard, Duke of Norfolk[21] (G.I. adm. 1561)	2
Lord Thomas Howard, Viscount Bindon, uncle of above (his third son, Thomas, M. T. adm. 1565)	1
Philip Howard, son of Duke of Norfolk	1
Sir George Howard, Master of the Armory in 1564 [Cal. State Papers, June 30, 1564] (G. I. adm. 1564?)	1
* Sir William Paulet, Marquis of Winchester, Lord Treasurer (G. I. adm. 1546)	1
Sir Hugh Paulet, related to above	1
a* Sir Walter Mildmay (G. I. adm. 1546)	2
* Sir Christopher Hatton (I. T. adm. 1561/2)	1
a* Sir William Herbert, Earl of Pembroke (I. T. adm. 1530)	2
Lady Ann Talbot (née Ann Herbert), dau. of above, dau.-in-law of *Earl of Shrewsbury	1
* Sir John Mason	1
Edward de Vere, Earl of Oxford (G. I. adm. 1566/7)	3
* Nicholas Wotton	1
Thomas Butler, Earl of Ormonde, a court favorite (G. I. adm. 1566/7)	1
Thomas Radcliffe, Earl of Sussex	1

[19] The names of patrons were taken from the DNB and title pages
(original editions and reprints).

[20] For meaning of abbreviations G. I., I. T., and M. T., see p. 129,
infra.

[21] Higginson has summarized the argument for the Duke of Norfolk's
Puritan sympathies, *Spenser's Shepherd's Calender,* pp. 54-57.

a* Sir Thomas Sackville, Lord Buckhurst (I. T. adm. 1555) 1
 Sir William Chester, Lord Mayor in 1560 (see also p. 140, *supra*) 1
 John Astley, Master of Queen's Jewel House, and John Harington 1
a Bishop Jewel 1
 Lawyers (Compton, 1; Lovelace, 2; Gawdy [I. T. 1549], 1; three others, 1) 5
 Others (Sir Thomas Kemp, Argall, St. Leger, Lady Hales, Bamfield, Lassels) 6

Total (one duplication excluded. See p. 141, *infra*) 69

* Indicates member of Queen's Privy Council or wife of a member. Warwick, Shrewsbury, Sackville, and Hatton were admitted subsequently to publication.

a Known to have Puritan proclivities or recognized as Puritan leaders.

Almost every book here represented was dedicated to a member of the Queen's Privy Council, to some member of his family, or to some other leading noble, all of whom with rare exceptions were prominent supporters of the Protestant cause and the new government. The dedications to Cecil, his wife, his sister-in-law, Lady Bacon, and Sir Nicholas Bacon, her husband, amount to ten; those to Leicester and persons closely related to him—his brother-in-law, the Earl of Huntingdon, his brother and sister-in-law, the Earl and the Countess of Warwick, and the Countess' father, the Earl of Bedford, an early and distinguished member of the reform party—sixteen; those to the Duke of Norfolk, for the time being a recognized leader of the Protestants, his son, his uncle, and Sir George Howard, five—in all thirty-one, or nearly half, and with those dedicated to the Queen added, considerably more than half, of the whole list. With two exceptions, the patrons who were members at the inns belonged either to Gray's Inn or the Inner Temple, Cecil's and Leicester's inns respectively. Books dedicated to members of the Privy Council constitute about two-thirds of the entire number.[22]

Cases of intimacy between the translators and their patrons, moreover, were frequent. Golding and Hall[23] (the latter from 1552) resided at Cecil's house. Googe, between whom and Turberville bonds of close friendship existed, was Cecil's kinsman, and was in his employ.[24] Hoby was Cecil's brother-in-law, and Wilson his old-time friend and neighbor. Drant may have been a frequent visitor in Cecil's home.[25] Studley was the Prime Minister's fellow-townsman and had attended the Westminster Grammar School, in the students of which Cecil took special interest.[26] The registration at Gray's Inn of Cecil's three wealthy wards[27] (during their minority) while members of his household, also indicates the Prime Minister's continued interest in his own inn, where many of the translators congregated. Leicester maintained even closer relations with the Inner Temple.[28] Churchyard, as a former member of the Earl of Surrey's household, had per-

[22] The number (5) dedicated to lawyers is significant, see p. 40, *supra*.

[23] Golding, *Metamorphoses*, Dedication, 1565; Wright, *Life and Works of Hall*, p. 20. As further evidence of the intimacy between the Prime Minister and the former of these two translators, be it noted that Golding's nephew and pupil, the young Earl of Oxford, on whose account Golding resided at Cecil's house, in 1571, married Cecil's daughter Anne. The friendly relations between Hall and both Sir William Cecil and the latter's son, Sir Thomas, were life-long.

[24] Letter by Cecil reprinted in Googe, *Eglogs* (Arber edition, p. 9).

[25] His first edition of Horace (1566) was dedicated to the Ladies Bacon and Cecil. The daughters of Sir Anthony Cooke, a reformer of note, the Ladies Cecil, Bacon, Hoby, and Killigrew, were distinguished for their learning.

[26] See *Agamemnon*, Dedication (Spearing edition, p. 20). *Cal. State Papers, Dom.*, 1564?, cite Latin verses addressed to Cecil by Studley, which suggest the continued friendship between them.

[27] The Earls of Oxford (1566/7) and Rutland (1566), and Arthur Hall (1556).

[28] See p. 26, *supra*, for services rendered by him to the Inn; no member was to be retained against him. Inderwick, *op. cit.*, lxii.

sonal claims on the Howards, noblemen of great prestige. Phaer recognized the Marquis of Winchester as his "firste brynger vp and patrone,"[29] and Norton was a literary collaborator with Sir Thomas Sackville,[30] later Lord Buckhurst.

To their patrons' friendliness and continued personal encouragement the translators give direct testimony. In the dedication of *Caesar*, Golding recalls the favorable reception which Cecil had given the *Warres of the Gothes* (1563) and refers with evident gratitude and esteem to "your accustomed goodnesse and gentelnesse towards me."[31] In the dedication of the first four books of the *Metamorphoses*, which he presented to Leicester as a New Year's gift (1565), he acknowledges the latter's favor,

whereby you are wont not onlye too beare with the want of skill and rudenesse of suche as commit their dooinges too your protection,[32] but also are woont too encourage them to proceede in their paynfull exercises.

Studley is likewise appreciative of Cecil's

hartye goodwill, and frendlie affection, that your honour bare towardes all studentes,[33]

and later citing the Earl of Bedford's "zeale in fauoring & furthering all learnynge & good Studies," adds the hope that his second patron will

[29] *Aeneid*, Dedication. The passage shows also that the Marquis of Winchester had recommended Phaer to Queen Mary for the position he held in the Marches of Wales.

[30] Sackville was named by Heywood among "Minerva's men." See p. 24, *supra*.

[31] *Cf*. Cecil's reception of Googe's work. *Zodiake of Lyfe*, 1565, Dedication. (Arber edition of Googe's *Eglogs*, p. 13.)

[32] In the expanded and versified form of this dedication (1567 edition) Golding indicates that Leicester's encouragement extends to all translators generally.

[33] *Agamemnon*, Dedication (Spearing edition, p. 20).

beare with my bould attempt, whervnto your Honors great cur-
tesie hath highly encouraged me to aspire.[34]

Turberville recalls the Countess of Warwick's earlier
favor to him,

so much the more abusing in mine owne conceite your Ladishippes
pacience, in that I had pardon before of my rash attempt.[35]

Dolman expresses his gratitude to Bishop Jewel as follows:

I thought it my dutye, in respecte of manye benefites, by your
lordship on me bestowed, to dedicate vnto you this my simple
trauayle.[36]

In view of their apparent sincerity, the specific character of their statements, and the high ideals professed
by them, the translators can hardly be accused of addressing their patrons merely to flatter them. Expectation
of gains either from sales[37] or gifts,[38] also, they strongly

[34] *Medea*, Dedication (Spearing edition, p. 124).

[35] *Epitaphes, Epigrams, Songes, and Sonets*, Dedication (Chalmers,
English Poets, 2:581).

[36] *Op. cit.*, Dedication.

[37] "Prayse I seke not for nor except I be a foole I care not for. To
doo that whych I doo, is and shalbe to me recompence sufficiente. I
neuer harde tell of anye man that was great gayner by poesies, and the
better the poet is, the more commonlye is he hated."—Drant, *Horace*,
"To the Reader," 1567 (*Jahrbuch der Deutschen Shakespeare Gesellschaft*, 47:54). *Cf.* p. 83, *infra*.

   "Yet seake I not herein to be copartener of his gayne."
        —Googe, *Zodiake of Lyfe*, 1561 (Arber edition of the *Eglogs*,
        p. 8).

[38] "I neyther gape for gaine nor greedie fee,
   My Muse and I haue done, if men in gree
   will take this trifling toye."
        —Turberville, *Heroycall Epistles*, "The Translator to his
        Muse."

   "No gredye golden fee, nor jem or jewell brave,
   But, of the reader, good reporte this writer longes to have."
        —*Ibid.*, verses in Fenton's *Certaine tragicall Discourses*, 1567
        (Tudor Translations, p. 14).

disavowed, the reward sought being not even fame[39] but "an immortall Crowne."[40] Rather, these frequently recurring citations of the patrons' friendliness to the various translators were deliberately designed to advertise to the public the sanction which the nobility were giving the translation movement.[41] Golding leaves little doubt on this score when he says, in the dedication of his *Calvin* (*Offences*) to the Earl of Bedford,

Not for that I thinke the matter cōteyned in this Booke needeth the defence of any man, . . . but because I truste that other shall be more willinge to receiue it, and vse it to their comforte &

> "Submit thy selfe to persons graue / whose Iudgement ryght alwayes . . .
> Whom no desyre of fylthy gayne / whom lucre none can moue
> From truth to stray."
>> —Neville, in Googe's *Eglogs* (Arber edition, p. 21).

[39] "Or as the proude enflamed with desyer
Of praise, and gape for glorious renoume . . .
But Studley prict with feruent harty zeale,
And vertues force preuailing in his mynd,
Regarding laude and honour neuer a deale."
　　—W. Parker, verses in Studley's *Agamemnon* (Spearing edition, p. 15, ll. 318-319, 326-327).

[40] "Farre easyer tis for to obtain, the Type of true Renowne.
Like Labours haue been recompenst / with an immortall Crowne."
　　　—Neville, in Googe's *Eglogs* (Arber edition, p. 23).

"The woork is brought too end by which the author did account
(And rightly) with eternall fame above the starres to mount."
　　　—Golding, *Metamorphoses*, Dedication, ll. 3-4.

"How wel did then hys freindes requite / his trauayle and hys paine,
When vnto hym they haue (as due) ten thousand thankes agayne?"
　　—T. B. verses in Studley's *Agamemnon* (Spearing edition, p. 16, ll. 348-351).

[41] The manner in which the nobility were lending their names for the sake of commending certain publications to the reading public is illustrated by a confessional tract by Queen Catherine Parr reissued in 1563 with the following superscription to the preface: "William Cicill hauing taken much profite by the readyng of this treatise folowyng, wisheth vnto euery Christian by the readinge thereof like profite with increase from God." Dibdin-Herbert-Ames, *Typographical Antiquities*, 4 : 572.

comoditie, when they see it after a sorte conueyed and commended vnto them, as it were from your Lordeships handes.[42, 43]

But why should the leading noblemen of the Elizabethan period take such an interest in the translation of the classics? Fortunately the reasons are not far to seek in the case of at least two sorts of ancient writings, and there are on record two instances of direct instigation of a translator by the Prime Minister, Cecil, to produce books belonging to these two classes.

Translations as Books of Warfare

FIRST, certain classics were regarded as valuable for instruction in warfare. With startling suddenness in the first part of the sixteenth century great changes had occurred in military science. In this department of human affairs, as in many others, that period was a transitional one. Feudal tactics generally had gone into the discard, and England in particular was behind the continent. In this emergency the highly developed methods of the ancients commended themselves. In 1539, when Cromwell was dreaming of a grand alliance against the Emperor, Morison translated Frontinus, the Roman strategist. In 1544, when Henry was at war with France, Cope translated Livy's account of the campaigns of Hannibal and Scipio, for

in the readyng thereof, men also may learne bothe to dooe displeasure to theyr ennemies, and to auoyde the crafty and daungerous baites, which shall be layde for theim.[44]

[42] See also Whitehorne, *Arte of Warre*, Dedication (Tudor Translations, p. 9); *cf. Scholemaster* (Arber edition, p. 79).

[43] For still another almost equally important reason for this appeal to influential patrons, see Chapter V, *infra*.

[44] Dedication.

Brend declared in 1553 that a nobleman might become "a man of warre the fyrste daye" through reading of the exploits of Alexander, who

began so young, and continued so smale tyme: yet no mans actes be comparable to his: beinge counted the most excellente captayne from the begynnyng.[45]

In Elizabeth's time, after the mismanagement of the previous reign, with the attendant loss of Calais, military knowledge was especially required for reorganizing the army against possible attacks by Scotland and Spain, and for protection from enemies at home who sought to overthrow the work of the reformation and the revolution. Aid of the Protestants in Germany even might have been contemplated. Accordingly, translations of five books pertaining to warfare were published shortly after the beginning of the reign: Barker's *Cyrus*, Whitehorne's *Arte of Warre* (Machiavelli) and *Onosandro Platonico, or the General Captayne;* Golding's *Commentaries of Julius Caesar;* and Sadler's *Vegetius*. Other translations that may have been intended for advancing knowledge of military matters were Watson's *Polybius* (1568), Fleming's *Aelianus* (1576), and Newton's *Rutilius Rufus* (1580).[46] Indeed books we might least suspect of having a bearing on warfare, the people of the sixteenth century in their anxious curiosity regarded seriously in that connection; even *Heliodorus* is said to have been "gravely considered a handbook of tactics."[47]

[45] *Quintus Curtius*, Dedication. Brend reports that Alexander slept with *Homer* under his pillow. See p. 61, *infra*. Smyth, on the authority of Cicero, cites the case of Lucius Lucullus, whose sole preparation for his victory over Mithridates was obtained from histories read while he was crossing the Mediterranean. Alexander Severus always prepared himself for war by the study of histories. *Herodian*, Dedication (1553).

[46] See complete titles in Palmer.

[47] Whibley, Tudor Translations, p. xiv.

But the reason assigned for the interest in these books rests upon more than mere inference. In that period the nations of Europe were receiving ocular demonstration of the worth of ancient military practices in the steady advances of the Turks upon the southeast. It was with this very circumstance actually in mind that Whitehorne, the translator of two of the books just cited, offered his *Onosandro Platonico* to the Duke of Norfolk, for he testifies that it was because they used the methods of antiquity that the Turks, whom he personally had observed in battle, were winning their great successes. Earlier, in his dedication of the *Arte of Warre* he had pointed out the active interest taken by the ancients in military matters and had argued that it was owing to the knowledge even of the "unarmed and rescalle people that followed the Campes" that the nations of antiquity had been delivered from the invader and that through the skill of the many "the Empire [had] continually inlarged and moste wonderfully and triumphantly prospered."

Caesar's *Commentaries* had a very practical significance for sixteenth century students of military affairs. In 1531 Elyot had recommended them as a handbook for waging war upon the Scots and the Irish,[48] and in 1588 they constituted the Spaniards' only source of topographical knowledge of the British Isles.[49] Brend, the translator of Quintus Curtius—án author who wrote of Alexander's campaigns—in 1564 was engaged upon the translation of this book, but died before he had accomplished the work, probably leaving the manuscript among his other effects at the Middle Temple. Evidently the loss thus incurred was looked upon by members of the

[48] *Gouernour*, 1:11.
[49] Preserved Smith, *History of the Reformation*, p. 341.

government as no trifling one, for Golding states[50] that Cecil brought the uncompleted book to him to finish. This act of the Prime Minister is notable, for, as D. Nichol Smith says, "the kind of book which Burghley favored had a direct bearing on the welfare of the state."[51] The apology made by Golding for his own ignorance of military matters indicates the kind of value put upon the *Commentaries*.

Part of the interest which the nobility took in the translation of the classics, therefore, might be considered as due to the supposed usefulness of certain books in the organization of the national defense.

Translations to Discourage Sedition

ANOTHER ground for interest in translations on the part of the Elizabethans was the reputed influence of the classics in allaying seditious tendencies. Among free peoples, a stronger safeguard against uprisings than military force is increased intelligence. The counter-revolution under Mary had served to show upon what unstable grounds the new order rested, and, besides, the situation was exceedingly complicated for the new government. Though succeeding under the terms of Henry's will, Elizabeth depended for her tenure upon the legality of the divorce granted by a Protestant court to Henry at the time of his separation from Catherine of Aragon, and in turn upon the continued success of the Protestant cause. Almost everything on the side of tradition was against her, so that the unthinking majority of her subjects would tend to renounce her as one who, according

[50] *Caesar*, Dedication.
[51] *Shakespeare's England*, 2:191.

to the Roman church, was of illegitimate birth—and hence unfitted to inherit the throne—in favor of some one deriving the right to rule out of the past, such as Philip of Spain or Mary, Queen of Scots.

Throughout the period of the translation movement— one in which the much-agitated question of the succession was continually to the fore—the hopes of the English Catholics rose and fell with the fortunes of Mary, who, as great-granddaughter of Henry VII, had assumed the arms and style of Queen of England. In three periods between 1559 and 1569 her claims were a source of real danger to Elizabeth. In 1560-1561, a French force, sent to put down an uprising of Scotch Protestants, to whom Elizabeth was giving substantial assistance, threatened to invade England and to place Mary on the throne. Her subsequent elusion of the English fleet and return to Scotland caused a new consternation. Once again, in 1565-1567, Mary threw off a temporary attitude of conciliation and frankly adopted a Catholic policy, this time successfully putting her Protestant subjects to flight. Finally in 1569, the Duke of Norfolk rashly sought the hand of the Scotch queen, now expatriated, and the Dukes of Westmoreland and Northumberland took the field in favor of her succession. Significantly or otherwise,[52] the large majority of the translations from the classics were produced in these three periods and in the years 1570-1571, when Spain was fitting out an expedition to invade England from the Netherlands, a papal bull was issued excommunicating Elizabeth, and a Catholic plot was set on foot to assassinate her. Thus it would

[52] The falling off of the translation activity in the years 1562-1564, when the dangers from France, Spain, and Scotland were wholly mitigated, is remarkable.

appear that in some way through the reading of classical literature the public were to be advised of the general misery and the national decline certain to be attendant upon civil strife.

Classical history had earlier been made use of several times for this purpose. Paynell in 1541, when Henry was facing a conspiracy headed by Sir John Neville, published the *Conspiracie of Catiline* with the avowed purpose of allaying sedition.[53] Suggestively enough, he republished it in 1557, when Mary's throne was tottering. Brend, too, at the end of Edward's troubled reign, and on the eve of the counter-revolution, had called attention to this advantage of books of history.[54]

In this connection the great importance laid upon Lucan's *Pharsalia* needs to be specially noted. The figure of Caesar, Lucan's hero, and one of the medieval "nine worthies," carried great prestige, and the story of the Roman civil wars appears to have possessed a fascination for the peoples of the time. The two attempts at this author—by Googe in 1560, when the new government was passing through its critical days, and by Turberville about 1570,[55] when the effort of the Rebels of the North to put Mary, Queen of Scots, upon the throne, had with difficulty been thwarted and the Papists were looking for help from Spain—are of interest not so much on account of the causes that led to their abandonment as for the reasons that prompted their beginning. Googe indicates that his work is directed against the malcontents among Elizabeth's subjects, when he represents his muse as saying,

[53] Dedication.
[54] Dedication.
[55] *Modern Philology*, 15:528.

Stand vp yong man, quoth she, dispatch, and take thy pen in
   hand,
  Wryte thou the ciuill warres and broyle in auncient Latines
    land.
Reduce to English sence, she said, the lofty Lucanes verse
  The cruel chaunce and dolfull end of Cesars state rehearse.[56]

Quite similarly Turberville in the days of the later crisis
in national affairs declares his purpose to be wholly a political one.

And shall I (Lady) be mislykte / to take in hande a deed,
By which vnto my natiue soyle / aduantage may succeede?
By which the ciuill swordes of Rome and mischiefes done thereby,
May be a myrror vnto vs, / the like mishappes to flie?[57]

The degree to which Lucan was considered a political
tract against sedition appears also from the reissuance of
a book entitled *The Serpent of Division*.[58] Originally written by Lydgate to counteract tendencies toward rebellion
in the reign of Henry VI, it was composed out of material
taken from Jehan de Tuim's *La Hystoire de Julius Cesar*,
which was in turn dependent upon Lucan. It was republished in 1559, almost coincident with Googe's attempt, and appeared once more in 1590 in the same volume with *Gorboduc*, which also had a political purpose.

Still another instance of the use of a classical translation to deter those inclined to rebellion was that of Ap-
pian, published in 1578, while Mary was still a prisoner

---

[56] *Zodiake of Lyfe*, Preface, 1560 (Arber edition of *Eglogs*, p. 7).

[57] *Tragicall Tales* (1587, p. 10), "The author declareth the cause why
he wrote these Histories and forewent the translation of the learned
Poet Lucane."

[58] "*The Serpent of Division*. Wherein is conteined the true History or
Mappe of Romes ouerthrowe, gouerned by Auarice, Enuye, and Pride,
the decayes of Empires, be they neuer so sure." Edited, with introduction, notes, and a glossary, by Henry Noble MacCracken, 1911.

in the hands of her cousin, Elizabeth. In the preface the following passage occurs:

How God plagueth them that conspire againste theyr Prince, this Historie declareth at the full. For of all them, that coniured against Caius Caesar, not one did escape violent death. The which this Author hathe a pleasure to declare, bycause he would affray all men from disloyaltie toward their Soueraigne.[59]

The title page also pointedly advertises the book as "an euident demonstration, That peoples rule must giue place, and Princes power preuayle."[60]

According to a story for which Dr. Johnson is said to be sponsor, in 1570, the year of threatened interference from Spain, Wilson, at the instance of the government, translated Demosthenes' orations to strengthen the country's morale.[61] This is a "curious" story, as Pollard remarks, yet the political purpose of the translation is clearly proclaimed on the title page,[62] and as Mair, Wilson's latest editor, remarks, "Philip of Macedon for the Englishman meant Philip of Spain, and the lesson was enforced by a comparison of Athens and England in the preface."[63] To one who has examined the contents of the book its propagandist nature is further apparent, for throughout the dedication, preface, and excerpts from

[59] W. B.

[60] For the continued interest in Caesar and the civil wars, see the lament for Pompey's wife in Howell's *Devises*, 1581.

[61] Pollard, DNB, article "Wilson."

[62] Wilson's *Arte of Rhetorique*, Introduction, p. xiii.

[63] "The three Orations of Demosthenes chiefe Orator among the Grecians, in fauour of the Olynthians, a people in Thracia, now called Romania: with those his fovver Orations titled expressely & by name against king Philip of Macedonie: most nedefull to be redde in these daungerous dayes, of all them that loue their Countries libertie, and desire to take vvarning for their better auayle, by example of others. Englished out of the Greeke by Thomas Wylson Doctor of the ciuill lavves."—Norton's title of his *Trogus* (1560?) reads, . . . "Orations, of Arsanes agaynst Philip the trecherous Kyng of Macedone. . . ."

other writers preceding the text, pointed references to
love of country and the duty of remaining loyal to it
abound, and several times allusion is directly made to the
contemporary disorders. Demosthenes is declared to be as
applicable to one age as another, as the case of an ambassador's actual use *verbatim* of one of this orator's orations
at the French court shows. Moreover, many analogies in
the conduct of the two Philips and of the national situations must have been apparent to the common people, to
whom very evidently the translation was chiefly addressed. The orator's encouragement, for example, to
meet the aggressions in spite of a depleted treasury must
have seemed very timely. The translator also stresses
need for obedience to magistrates, deference of the com-
mons to their superiors, and support of the established
religion. An oath which the young Grecians were said to
have taken appears among the prefatory matter, in which
those who took it declared, "I will euermore honor the
religion of Countrie." Following the oath occurs this
comment,

Such care had these heathen people to the prosperous safegarde
of their Nation, much to the shame and confusion of all these in
our dayes that are common traytors and open Rebels to their
naturall soyle and Countrie.

Finally the volume ends, as if the passage were part of
the original, with this commentary upon the "most cruel
& miserable death" of Demades,

A worthie ende for all such whatsoeuer they be, that are wicked
betrayers of their naturall soyle and Countrie, who after a sort
plucke out their owne bowelles, in that they alienate from themselues to others (whatsoeuer the respect be) the proper inherit-
aunce and birth right of their owne nation, the chiefest and
greatest treasure belonging to man vpon earth, next to the true
knowledge and reuerent feare of God.

There can remain small doubt that Wilson, himself a political appointee of the government, worked under Cecil's specific direction.

Other important reasons for the nobility's interest in the translation of classical writings will be discussed in the next chapter.

CHAPTER IV

PRINCIPLES AND ISSUES OF THE MOVEMENT

THE middle ages are commonly styled the ages of faith—faith, it might almost be said, in an eternal calm. Through the narrow perspective of that period the fundamental character of the world appeared never to change, either physically or spiritually. The low-hung heavens remained enclosed in their crystalline spheres, studded with stars. Wars were waged by divinely commissioned, absolute rulers without heed to the laws of society or of nations, which, through their relation to a factitious *universal*, were regarded as static. Curiosity and imagination were closely fettered, so that to investigate natural laws or entertain new conceptions of warfare, the state, the church, the office of the Bishop of Rome, the tenets of the theologians, the processes of the logicians, or private or public morals, was not to be attempted or tolerated.

On the other hand, classical literature, with its appeal to reason and the imaginative faculty, presented to the men of the renaissance an array of differing conceptions concerning all matters under the sun, which no amount of dialectic philosophy could harmonize and which usually were directly antithetical to the thought of the middle ages and the doctrines of the church. Classical histories not only revealed the passage of time but told of the rise and fall of great nations and empires in lands hitherto beyond the ken of the peoples of western Europe. These histories also told of free peoples who preferred death to loss of personal liberty. The ancient philosophers and scientists expressed faith in the laws of nature, and the ancient poets were unrestrained in creating figments of the imagination, inexpressibly charming, or in enunciating principles of moral conduct operative above any temporal authority. At these discoveries thought and the reasoning faculties were both staggered and stimulated. The old scholars, grounded during their youth in tradition, when reading classical literature, attempted not to be distracted by its teachings and implications, yet they foresaw in a vulgar familiarity with it the inevitable downfall of all their systems and institutions. The new generation,—whose rise in England may be considered as roughly coincident with the latter part of Henry's reign and the time of the subsequent revolution,—naturally restive under the restraint of an effete order, were thrilled with the new view of the world.

With the sudden success of the renaissance in Edward's reign, far-seeing members of the nation presently recognized in translations of the classics instruments for setting up the new order. To remove the danger to the reformation and the revolution, due to the presence of sympathizers with the old institutions, the new nobility, created by the Tudors, sought to introduce the rationalistic spirit of ancient literature as the most direct means of transforming national ideals. Only through an intelligent public opinion, created to displace abject reverence for authority and immemorial custom, could the ecclesiastical schisms which had arisen in the sixteenth century be justified, and the stabilization of the new government and a vigorous national growth be assured.

Point of View of the Youth Movement

SINCE the days of the first humanists, rationalism had been slowly permeating the nation. Plato, among other influences, proved to be an author stimulating to new forms of thought. More and Erasmus had regarded him among their favorite authors, and he had been introduced into the universities. Cheke, Ascham, Cecil,[1] and many others had found stimulation in his works. As time went on, Plutarch and the republican Cicero taught to many sweet reasonableness and—skepticism.[2] The historians and in turn Seneca began to affect political and moral theory. Other strong liberalizing influences came through the renaissance writers of France and Italy, notably the French reformer, Peter Ramus, who in 1536 startled the Sorbonne and the world with his thesis, *Quaecumque ab Aristotle dicta essent, commentitia esse*. His vogue presently spread to England, his works were to be found in private libraries, like that of Sir Thomas Smith at Hill House,[3] and he came to be greatly looked up to by the Puritans of Cambridge because he was a Calvinist.[4]

The power which the classics exerted and the delight

[1] *Cf.* Ascham, *Scholemaster*, p. 47 and *passim* (Arber edition).

[2] No translation of Plato was made in the sixteenth century, but Plutarch and Cicero both appeared several times before 1550. Among the Elizabethan translators, Heywood (*Hercules Furens*, Dedication, de Vocht edition, p. 200) and North (*Diall of Princes*, Dedication, 1557) specifically mention Plato, and Dolman cites him as the source of some of his advanced views (see p. 31, *supra*). Howell refers to Ficino [Ficius], the neo-Platonist (Corser, *Collecteana*, Pt. 9:103), and Golding quotes Philo of Alexandria (*Metamorphoses*, Dedication, 1567, ll. 354-370), who had been rendered into Latin by Humphrey, the Cambridge scholar, and into English by Grimald(?) in 1563. *Cf.* Elyot's enthusiasm for Plato and Cicero (*op. cit.*, 1:11). Of course, during the whole renaissance period Cicero was the strongest classical influence.

[3] Strype, *Life of Sir Thomas Smith* (1820), Appendix Number VI.

[4] Mullinger, *University of Cambridge*, 2:411.

which they afforded are manifest in the testimony of the translators. Dolman found in Cicero's *Tusculanae*

suche profyte, and pleasure therin, as it were not possible to finde the like in anye Ethnike wryter,[5]

and Studley recommends Seneca as something to be prized more

then y[e] rich Iewels and somes of gold & siluer, y[t] wor[l]dly minds do vse to gratifie their frends withal.[6]

Heywood in his preface to *Thyestes* devoted nearly a hundred and fifty lines to a description of Parnassus, where the garnished volume of his author was the joy of the Muses,[7] and the enthusiasm expressed in the commendatory verses prefixed to Studley's *Agamemnon* is infectious. Slightly different evidence of the force with which the renaissance ideals gripped the translators' generation is to be found in the play upon the word "reason" in Neville, Googe, Golding, and others. Only men of reason, they said, could be trusted;[8] reason advised in hours of depression;[9] frequently, though unfortunately not always, it governed in matters of love;[10] it distinguished man from brute;[11] it controlled the will and sub-

[5] Dedicatory "Epistle."
[6] *Medea*, Dedication (Spearing edition, p. 123).
[7] Ll. 505 ff. (de Vocht edition, pp. 110 ff.).
[8] "Submit thy selfe to persons graue, / whose Iudgement ryght alwayes
    By Reason rulde doth ryghtly iudge, / whom Fancies none can charme,
    Which in most Inconstant brains, / are chyefly wont to swarme."
                            —Neville, in Googe's *Eglogs* (Arber edition, p. 21).
[9] Googe, *ibid.*, p. 107.
[10] *Ibid.*, p. 106. Love was subject for radical disagreement between the translators and writers not in sympathy with the renaissance. See pp. 78, 79, *infra*.
[11] *Ibid.*, pp. 102-104. The writer laments that the little bird Marly lacks reason.
    "Now looke how long this clod of clay too reason dooth obey,
    So long for men by just desert account our selves wee may."
                            —Golding, *Metamorphoses*, "To the Reader," ll. 109-110.

dued the appetite;[12] it was the means of relationship with
God[13] and the law of individual conduct;[14] the possession
of reason would bring contentment;[15] and reason was the
force by which the individual and the commonwealth was
to be ruled.[16]

Therefore the translation of Latin or Greeke authours, doeth
not onely not hinder learning, but it furthereth it, yea it is learning it self, and a great staye to youth, . . . and a vertuous exercise for the unlatined to come by learning, and to fill their minde
with the morall vertues, and their body with civyll condicions,
that they maye bothe talke freely in all company, live uprightly
though there were no lawes, and be in a readinesse against all

[12] "If reason cannot rule thy wil,
But vice wil reign through appetite,
Then let the harmes, that happen stil
Through lusts, refrain thy fond delight."
—I.A., 1566, *A Collection of Seventy-nine Black Letter Ballads*,
Joseph Lilly, editor, p. 101.

"The office of the minde, is to haue power
Uppon the bodye, and to order well
The bodys office yeke in euery hower.
It is of the minde to lerne the perfite skyll
The vayne desyres that rise, him by to kill
Wherby the mynde dothe kepe his perfite strength
And yeke the bodye vanquishe loste at length."
—H[owell], *Fable of Narcissus*. (Quoted in Corser, *op. cit.*, Pt.
9:102.)

"But Appetite, which reason doth despise,
Mysseleadeth not a few."—Sanford, *Plutarch*, "To the Reader."

[13] "Our soule is wee, endewed by God with reason from above:
Our bodie is but as our house, in which we woorke and move."
—Golding, *op. cit.*, ll. 103-104.

[14]   "But such as are under awe
Of reasons rule continually doo live in vertues law."
—*Ibid.*, Dedication, ll. 59-60.

[15] "Sciences, say they [the ancient philosophers] prepare mens mindes
to vertue . . . Yea, Science and knowledge are the very seminary or
seedes out of which do bud all our florishing blossoms of vertue, and
wherein our sprites are made hable to iudge of highe and hard thinges,
and so raised to those holy desires of well dooing, wherein all good men
repose their soueraigne contentment."—Fenton, *Golden Epistles*, 1575.

[16] *Cf.* Elyot, *op. cit.*, 1:14 (end). See Bavand, p. 37, *supra.*

kinde of worldlye chaunces that happen, whiche is the profite that commeth of Philosophy.[17]

Having adopted such 'radical' views, the new order undertook to dethrone reverence for tradition and attacked the whole structure of medieval institutions at its base in order to clear the ground for a new civilization.

The Influence of Histories

THE men of the renaissance and the translators in particular stressed the liberalizing effect of historical study.[18] It should be recalled that in the sixteenth century almost any relation, whether of fact or fiction, was included under the term history—Homer, Ovid, Seneca, the Greek romancers, and even Bandello, according to the standard of the time, being as significant as Livy or Quintus Curtius.[19] This inclusion is comprehensible when the renaissance theory of the office of history is considered, namely, to teach by means of examples how an individual might "apprehende" that which is "commodious" and "eschue that thing which . . . appeareth noisome and

[17] Hoby, *Courtier*, Dedication (Tudor Translations, p. 9).

[18] See Elyot's *Gouernour* (1531), *The Institution of a Gentleman* (1555, attributed to Grimald), and various dedications and prefaces, *passim*.

The interest in astronomy among the translators hardly competed with that of history. In 1535 Poyntz had translated Cebes, and some unknown person, Ptolemy. Salisbury in 1550 published his *Description of the Sphere or Frame of the Worlde*, rendered from Proclus. Googe attempted Aratus about 1560. Geography aroused slightly greater enthusiasm. Elyot had advocated the study of it (*op. cit.*, 1:11); and Brend, Smyth, Haward, and Golding (*Trogus*, Dedication, *Metamorphoses*, "To the Reader," ll. 200-204) pointed out the pleasure to be derived from reading of foreign lands. In 1571, Golding may have been contemplating the translation of Mela Pomponius, which did not appear until 1590 (*Psalms*, Dedication). Twyne's *Dionysus* (1572), "very necessary and delectable for students of Geographie, Saylers and others" (t. p.), and Alday's (?) *Pliny* are further evidence of the romantic interest in distant parts.

[19] *Cf.* Elyot, *op. cit.*, 3:25 (end).

vicious."[20] In other words, the whole body of narrative and dramatic literature was regarded much as we look upon novels, as stories representative of life in its details. Experience was being substituted for precepts, and principles for superstition and authority. Thus Brend, who commends Alexander, his classical author's hero, for his assiduous reading of Homer, in offering his translation of Quintus Curtius to his patron, says,

In theym [*i.e.*, histories] there be presydentys for all cases that may happē, in followyng the good, in eschuyng the euyl, in auoydyng incōuenyences, & in foreseyng mischiefes. . . . As in all artes there be certeyne prynciples and rules for men to folowe, so in hystoryes there be ensamples paynted out of all kynde of vertues wherin both the dignitye of vertue, & foulenes of vyce appeareth much more lyuelye then in eny morall teachyng: there beyng expressed by way of ensample, all that Philosophy doth teach by waye of precepts.[21]

But history interpreted in this manner came to have an application to public as well as private affairs. In the first part of the sixteenth century, renaissance education had been directed toward the training of noblemen both as individuals and as governors,[22] chiefly, however, it would seem, for handling isolated situations, little or no regard being had for broad policies or essential principles.

[20] Elyot, *op. cit.*, 3:25 (beginning).

[21] "Historiographers . . . haue put before our eyes the tymes, maners and doinges, of all sortes of men wᵗʰ theyr counselles, fortunes, and aduentures, the whyche theyr posteritie maye, as in a paynted Table beholde: and thereby learne to profyte, as well the Common wealthe, as their owne priuate estate."—Smyth, *Herodian* (1553), Dedication.

[22] Elyot, *op. cit.*, 1:6; 3:25 (beginning); *cf. The Institution of a Gentleman* (without pagination), section on histories. "Such histories then, are a treasure whiche neuer ought to be refused nor reiected oute of noble and learned handes, for by the diligent turnynge and readynge of them, they may be as profitable vnto the commō weale, as to them selues, theyr frendes, and priuate families and therwith haue an exacte knowlege of all that is necessarye to be knowen, concernynge thinges done in tymes past."—Paynell, *Darius*, Dedication.

Later, particularly by the time of the revolution, the application of history became extended, and there arose a quite modern view of the state. The first stage in the development of such a philosophy of history was manifested in an appreciation of the power of historical study to make one consider the administration of government a matter for sound reason and not for the self-willed and haphazard opportunism of princes; for Brend also says in the same exceedingly interesting dedication of *Quintus Curtius*, addressed to the Duke of Northumberland, then head of the state,

Then such as be wel experte in hystories . . . must nedes obteygne profoūdnes of iudgement, with a stable and groūded wysedome. . . . Thys is suche a thyng, that who so euer is clerely voyde of it, though he be endued wyth neuer so great a wytte otherwise; with such aptnes of nature or other goodly vertues. Yet when he shall haue to do in weyghtye affaires, he shall fynde a certeigne mayme and imperfection, not onely in ciuyll gouerment, but also in the matters perteining to the warre.

Further, the contemplation of long stretches of time revealed in histories induced an evaluation of the social forces upon which governments rest. By comparing "thynges past with thynges presente" and "waiyng the times wyth the causes and occasions of thynges," Brend arrived at the organic nature of the state, which was his initial thesis, stated at the beginning of his dedication.

"For in them [histories]," he says, "men may see the groundes and beginnynges of cōmen wealthes, yᵉ causes of their encrease, of their prosperous mayntenaūce, and good preseruation: and againe by what meanes they decreased, decayed, and came to ruyne."[23]

[23] James Colyn, Nicolls' intermediate French translator of Thucydides, professing to be of the school of Comines, sometimes called the father of modern history, had already expressed the same view, which Nicolls, friend of the liberal scholar Cheke, had taken the pains to render into English (1550).

Such a change of attitude toward the essential character of the state augured profound results. This attitude
once universally accepted, a distinct national life would
ensue. Citizens and nobles would no longer be considered
the sovereign's pawns; international embroilments and
continental expeditions for foreign conquest, the defense
of antiquated claims to foreign soil, or opposition to the
Emperor would not unadvisedly be entered into; rival
factions seeking to seize the throne would find themselves
bereft of followers; and general coöperation of the entire
body politic would be secured.

In 1553 the work of the revolution was suddenly interrupted and at the beginning of Elizabeth's reign the
rationalistic interpretation of history had so far been accepted that it was not necessary for the authors of dedications and prefaces in later translations of strictly historical works,[24] though they expressed a deep sense of loyalty
to country, to add anything to the theory of the political
value of history.

But the liberal historical tradition found voice also in
the *Mirror for Magistrates*, which, owing to the identity
or the close association of its authors[25] with the translators, may not here be overlooked. The renaissance interest
of the authors is evidenced by classical citations scattered
throughout the work; likewise Bishop Gardiner's earlier
interdiction of its publication[26] stamps it as representa-

[24] Besides the earlier translations by Cope, Nicolls, Smyth, Paynell,
and Brend (see pp. 22, 45, *supra*), Eutropius was translated by Haward
(1564), Bruni (Aretine, *Warres of the Gothes*) (1563), Trogus Pompeius (1564), and Caesar (1565) by Golding, and a section of Trogus
Pompeius by Norton (1564). The continued popularity of the pre-
Elizabethan translations is noteworthy. See p. 19 n., *supra*.

[25] All but one of the authors were members at the inns. Baldwin and
Sackville are named in Heywood's list of "Minerva's men"; Chaloner,
Dolman, and Churchyard translated classics.

[26] Haslewood edition, 2:1:5.

tive of the advanced views. Like Nicolls' dedication,[27] this book contains a protest against the flattering, ostentatious writings of the medieval historians (probably the authors of romances and possibly some of the chroniclers),[28] and the whole composition is based upon the exemplary theory of history, set forth both for public and private application. It views the long course of time and the attendant demolition of institutions, and in true renaissance fashion advertises fortune to be the supreme power in human affairs, above that of kings and prelates.

Thus the Earl of Salisbury begins his tale with the following words of discouragement to ambitious princes,

> What fooles bee we to trust vnto our strength,
> Our wit, our courage, or our noble fame,
> Which time it selfe must nedes deuour at length,
> Though froward fortune could not foile the same:
> But seeing this goddesse guideth all the game,
> Which still to chaunge doth set her onely lust,
> Why toyle wee so for thinges so harde to trust?[29]

The story that follows, like many another before and after it, must have proved exceedingly stimulating to the reasoning faculties of its readers, and its thesis that, though disaster comes at times to those who attempt to do the right, time ultimately exonerates them, must have furnished substantial encouragement for a cause that had just emerged from the Marian rigors.

Direct warnings against the abuse of authority appear in several narratives, as in the story of Richard II's dethronement by his subjects. This unhappy ruler declares,

> The king, which erst kept the realme in doute,
> The veriest rascall now dare checke and floute.[30]

[27] See p. 70 n., *infra*.
[28] Haslewood edition, 2:1:250-251.
[29] *Ibid.*, 2:1:90-96.
[30] *Ibid.*, 2:1:57.

Similarly Buckingham bemoans his fate,

> Who trusts too much to honour's highest throne,
> And warely watch not sly dame fortune's snares:
> Or who in court will beare the swinge alone,
> And wisely weigh not how to wield the care,
> Beheld hee me, and by my death beware.[31]

These few examples, selected from many of like import, were properly the reflections of a people who had just placed upon the throne a queen whose power rested upon her people's will.

Finally, a book which shows how completely the governmental leaders of the new régime accepted the new view of the state is Wilson's *Demosthenes*, which, though not a history, may be here treated as such. This book, published just after the Catholic uprising in 1569, and, as has been stated, during the Spanish crisis, was begun in 1556, probably at Cheke's suggestion, certainly under his influence. In it occur reminiscences of Cheke's regard for Demosthenes and of his zeal for inculcating a love of the classics within the minds of the fugitives gathered at Padua during the Marian persecutions, for the sake of inspiriting them in a time of political and ecclesiastical reverses. A noteworthy feature of the book is the amount of attention given in the introductory portions to the common people,[32] and the following sentence indicates that Wilson, Cheke, and Cecil, to the last of whom the book

[31] Haslewood edition, 2 : 1 : 333.

[32] *E.g.*, "And were it not better & more wisedome to speake plainly & nakedly after the common sort of men in few words, than to ouerflowe wyth vnnecessarie and superfluous eloquence as Cicero is thought sometimes to doe. . . . Well I had rather follow his [Demosthenes'] veyne, the whych was to speake simply and plainly to the common peoples vnderstanding, than to ouerflouryshe wyth superfluous speach, although I might thereby be counted equall with the best that euer wrate English."—Preface, fol. 9a.

was dedicated and at whose behest it was published (all three of them prominent liberals during the Edwardian régime) looked to the people for the support of their cause.

Moreouer he [Cheke] was moued greatly to like Demosthenes aboue all others, for that he sawe him so familiarly applying himselfe to the sense and vnderstanding of the common people, that he sticked not to say, that none euer was more fitte to make an English man tell his tale praise worthily in any open hearing, either in Parlament or in Pulpit, or otherwise, than this onely Orator was.[33]

It would seem that Cecil and his political confrères had accepted the new view of the nature of the state, and believing that classical literature tended to persuade others to adopt it, put their dependence upon it as one of the means of defeating the exponents of medieval absolutism and tradition, making secure the fruits of the revolution, and arousing a general national consciousness.

Arousing National Consciousness

For hundreds of years previous to the renaissance, the world had been united in a single church, had given allegiance, in theory at least, to one Emperor, and had carried on intercourse through the common medium of Latin. In contrast to this medieval devotion to universals, the men of the renaissance throughout western Europe, conceived aspirations for separate nationality. Yet in England, after the despotic reigns of Henry and Mary and the disastrous wars with France, national pride was at an especially low ebb, though out of the defeats had come the disguised blessing of once for all being rid of feudal ambitions for continental possessions on French soil.

[33] Dedication.

When intellectual inventory was taken, owing to the exclusive attitude toward learning, England found herself culturally far behind other western nations. To the sympathizers with the renaissance this was a painful reflection. Hence, the nobles and the translators, the latter of whom had democratically pledged their services not so often to prince as to country,[34] sought to arouse a national self-consciousness through an increased knowledge of ancient culture and the development of the mother tongue. The new men often chided the scholars for their neglect of duty in not translating the ancients and the renaissance writers, and looked forward to the time when through their own efforts the country would "at length flowe with the workes of philosophye"[35] and the English language would rival the learned tongues.

Brend[36] and Lord Morley[37] had early sounded a warning concerning the comparatively slow progress of English culture, and Hoby in 1561 dwelt more at length than either of the former writers on the subject. After stating that he knew not by what destiny Englishmen were much surpassed by almost all other nations in the matter of translating the classics, he contrasted with the exclusive and individual interests of his countrymen the pleasure and the friendly rivalry manifested by the schol-

[34] See pp. 35-37, *supra.*

[35] Dolman, *op. cit.*, Dedication.

[36] "I therefore hauyng alwayes desired that we englishmē might be founde as forwarde in that behalfe as other nations which haue brought all worthie histories into their naturall language, did a fewe yeares paste attempte the translacion of Quintus Curtius, and lately vpon an occasion performed & accomplished the same."—*Curtius*, Dedication.

[37] "Consyderynge that aswel in French, as in the Italyan (in the whyche both tongues I have some lytle knowledge) there is no excellente worke in the latyn, but that strayght wayes they set it forth in the vulgar."—Henry Parker, Lord Morley, *Triumphes of Fraunces Petrarcke*, Dedication (1553? M. A. Scott), Roxburghe Club, pp. 4-5.

ars abroad in rapidly turning all sorts of writings, especially Latin and Greek books of science and philosophy, into the various vernaculars. In translating the *Courtier* he had done as well as he was able, he said, and

even so coulde I wishe with al my hart, profounde learned men in the Greeke and Latin shoulde make the lyke proofe, and everye manne store the tunge accordinge to hys knowledge and delite above other men, in some piece of learnynge, that we alone of the worlde maye not bee styll counted barbarous in oure tunge, as in time out of minde we have bene in our maners. And so shall we perchaunce in time become as famous in Englande, as the learned men of other nations have ben and presently are.[38]

Evidence of the commitment of the entire company of translators and the nobles to this ideal, is contained in Golding's first dedication of the *Metamorphoses* to Leicester, who was, we are told, "woont too encourage" writers under his protection

to proceede in their paynfull exercises attempted of a zeale and desyre too enryche their native language with thinges not hertoofore published in the same.

Phaer, who rejoiced in being among the first to give a work of poetry to his countrymen, shows the process by which culture was to be improved.

If now the yong writers will vouche-saue to enter: they may finde in this language, both large and aboundant Campes of varietie, wherein they maie gather innumerable sortes, of most beautifull floures, figures, and phrases . . . to garnishe al kindes of their owne verses with a more cleane and compendious order of meter, than heretofore cōmonly hath ben accustomed.[39]

Judged by modern standards of originality, the mere furnishing of models to copy seems like setting low ideals

---

[38] *Courtier*, Dedication, *op. cit.*, p. 9. See also Golding, *Trogus*, "To the Reader." *Cf.* Whitehorne, *Arte of Warre*, Dedication (Tudor Translations, p. 8).

[39] *Aeneid*, Preface.

of literary excellence, but such a method has always proved a successful practice with beginners, and knowledge of "the best that has been thought and said" is usually prerequisite to further advancement. In this stage of national culture the chief object was to permeate the intellectual life of the nation with classical ideals.

Another way to arouse national consciousness was to secure respect—hitherto unknown—and a place of dignity in the public esteem for the English language.

After the late World War, the nations rehabilitated insisted upon a return to their own languages as part of the process of securing freedom from the domination of other peoples. Even more significantly, in the sixteenth century the declaration of the validity of English for all uses was the assertion of the principle of nationality against the whole force of the medieval belief in universals and absolutism. So great was the current prejudice against English that the translators at first regarded the employment for literary purposes of "our corrupt & base, or as al men affyrme it: most barbarous Language,"[40] as little more than experimental. English was thought, and perhaps rightly at that time, not to have the flexibility of Latin;

Thys our englishe toong (as many thinke and J here fynde) is farre vnable to compare with the latten,

wrote Heywood.[41] In spite, however, of misgivings on the part of several of them, the translators continued with

[40] Neville, *Oedipus*, Dedication, 1563. In the *Tenne Tragedies of Seneca* (1581), Neville's preface was reprinted and this passage was made to read "or as some men (but vntruly) affyrme it."
"My countrey language (whiche I haue heard discommended of many, and estemyd of some to be more than barbarous)."—Phaer, *Aeneid*, "To Good Readers," 1558.

[41] *Troas*, "To the Reader," 1559 (de Vocht edition, p. 7). "Consydre the grosenes of oure owne Coûtrey language, whiche can by no means aspire to the hyghe lofty Latinists Stile."—Phaer, Preface, 1563.

their work, though the pressure that was continually being exerted upon them is shown in Roll's argument written as late as 1574, on a closely related question.

Shall we then thinke that the Scottyshe or Englishe tongue, it [is] not fitte to wrote [write] any arte into? no in dede. But peraduenture thou wylt saye that there is not Scottyshe wordes for to declare and expresse all thinges contayned into liberall artes, truthe it is: neither was there Latin wordes to expresse all thinges writen in the Hebrewe and Greke tongues.[42]

Not only did the translators in the spirit of loyal Englishmen support the national movement by remaining faithful to their country's language, but they insisted upon having it used in its purity. The so-called "colores,"[43] that system of rhetorical tricks and flourishes upon which writers of medieval Latin spent untold time without contributing anything of value to thought or life,[44] and "ink-horn terms,"[45] or learned words imported from Latin—the two together constituting the elements of "eloquence"—the translators refused to employ,[46] for just as simplicity and directness of expression represented to them a desire for truth, general enlightenment, and national development, so the aureate pedantic style of the medievals betokened effeteness, exclusiveness, and anti-nationalism. Thus Dolman

[42] *Logicke*, "Epistle to the Reader."

[43] Berdan, *Early Tudor Poetry*, pp. 130 ff.

[44] "Whylest they desyred and coueyted fame of learning, and wente aboute to plante and establish theyr name to be continued from the iniurye of forgettynge: they bestowed theyr laboure, more in adournynge, garnyshinge and fylyng of their woordes, then in serchynge and declaryng of the trouth, thinking that, if any thynge of vntrouthe were by them set fourthe in causes, that were of long antiquitye before theyr tyme, it could not be corrected, and yet neuerthelesse, that they shulde perceyue exceadynge fruict and benefyte through that the delycatenes of theyr vayne narratyons, labours, and wyttes." Nicolls, *op. cit.*

[45] Wilson, *Arte of Rhetorique* (Mair edition, pp. 162-164).

[46] Dolman, *op. cit.*, Preface.

had rather to be partener of the fauour, due to simplicity, and plainenes; then, with foolyshe and farre fet wordes, to make my translatiō seeme more darke to the vnlearned, & more foolishe to the wise. . . . Thus muche I am sure of, that I haue thereby escaped, the iust reproofe, that they deserue, which thinke, to cloke their ignoraunce, wyth inkehorne termes;[47]

Adlington

used more common and familiar woords (yet not so muche as I might doo) for the plainer settinge foorth of the same;[48]

and Golding preferred

too lay foorth things plainlye (yea and sometimes also homely and grossely) too the vnderstanding of many, than too indyte things curyously too the pleasing of a fewe.[49]

This insistence of the translators that the classics be rendered without compromise into perfectly plain, current English, not merely served to give the vernacular a place of proper dignity; in principle, it permanently transferred the seat of authority in matters political and intellectual from a special class with an international, foreign outlook to the whole English public. Although the "new men" failed to thwart entirely the effort to latinize the language, as our present vocabulary, when compared with their native "homespun," shows, they established a principle necessary for independent national existence and future progress in culture. The increased respect for the mother tongue and the increased national *esprit de corps* are reflected in 1575 in the words of one who had formerly felt called upon to apologize for English.

[47] *Op. cit.* Dolman had to meet complaints against his "lacke of years and eloquence." His spirited defense of his youth is to be found on p. 31, *supra.*

[48] *Apuleius*, "To the Reader" (Seccombe edition, p. xxxviii).

[49] *Psalms*, Dedication.

It would pricke neere the learned tungs in strength,
Perchaunce and match mee some of them at length.[50]

Four years later the *Shepheardes Calender* appeared to
fulfil this prophecy, and presently the public morale was
sufficient for planting vigorous colonies beyond the seas,
resisting the aggressions of Spain, and inaugurating the
greatest period of productivity in the history of English
literature.

The Translators and the Reformation

THE translators were also of service to their country as
supporters of the reformation. For a short time after the
beginning of Elizabeth's reign, the disagreements that
have since divided the English church were not apparent.
The ecclesiastical leaders, just returned from contact with
the continental reformers, favored Calvinism, a bond between them and the translators. The course which the
government was to take in religious matters was not yet
revealed; and many hoped for a non-ritualistic discipline.
Considerable impatience was expressed at the dilatoriness
of the political leaders in declaring their ecclesiastical
program, yet the civil government was generally believed
to be in complete harmony with the extreme Protestant
cause. Likewise, Puritanism,[51] later antagonistic both to

[50] Golding, verses in Baret's *Alvearie*.

This prophecy, it should be said, is based on the proviso that English
be cleansed
"from the noysome weede
Of affectation which hath ouergrowne
Ungraciously the good and natiue seede,
As for to borrow where wee haue no neede."
Cf. Turberville in Gascoigne's *Posies*, 1575 (Hazlitt edition, 1 : xl).

[51] The denotation of the term Puritanism is of course a shifting one.
In this passage and earlier it indicates doctrines in harmony with those
of the Swiss reformers and opposition to Roman ritual. The separatist
movement began in 1566 with the expulsion by the Establishment of
about seventy clergymen for non-conformity. For later developments, see
p. 118, *infra*. The word Calvinism is used in the broad, inclusive sense.

Anglicanism and culture, was the profession of numbers of the nobility.

Upon one point in particular many were agreed: that Roman Catholicism had exerted its influence upon the nation by fostering ignorance. In Mary's time,

> No lore was taught to fyl the mynde,
> Godly to lyue, and good fruite reape,
> But al for Church they cride and threape.[52]

Bishop Jewel, Dolman's patron, repeatedly bemoaned the state of affairs. Oxford was wasted with ignorance and irreligion,[53] he said, and the English clergy were "no better than mere logs of wood without talent, or learning, or morality."[54] Everywhere there was "a profound silence respecting schools and the encouragement of learning,"[55] and "no care whatever" was being "taken for the encouragement of literature and the due succession of learned men."[56] Conversely, it is clear that Jewel believed that intellectual stimulation produced by classical literature would aid greatly in remedying the evils due to Papistry and the recent disorders.

Further, the reformation was a moral as well as a religious metastasis, its supporters strongly resisting the notion of a divorce of religion and life that had found a place in the medieval church. Man, according to the Protestant view of the sixteenth century, is of a twofold nature, spirit and brute, the intellectual faculties being a manifestation of the spirit.[57] Ignorance, therefore, "that

---

[52] *A Collection of Seventy-nine Black Letter Ballads*, Joseph Lilly, editor, p. 96.

[53] *Zurich Letters*, March 20, 1559.

[54] *Ibid.*, November 5, 1559.

[55] *Ibid.*, April 28, 1559.

[56] *Ibid.*, November 5, 1559.

[57] James Colyn, in Nicolls' *Thucydides*. The vital relationship that was felt to obtain between Protestantism and classical literature is mani-

whiche maketh vs lyke vnto beastes,"[58] menaced, at one and the same time, religion and all public and private morals as well; and since the country was considered to be in the throes of sordidness and crime,[59] the translators were thought to be able to render great aid in purifying national life. Certainly so much may be implied from the words of Neville:

Marke thou rather what is ment by the whole course of the Historie: and frame thy lyfe free from suche mischiefs, wherwith the worlde at this present is vniuersally ouerwhelmed, The wrathfull vengeaunce of God prouoked, The Bodye plaged, the mynde and Conscience in midst of deepe deuourynge daungers most terrybly assaulted, In suche sort that I abhorre to write: And euen at the thought therof I tremble and quake for very inward griefe and feare of minde, assuredly perswadinge my selfe that the ryght hyghe and immortall God, wyll neuer leaue suche horrible and detestable Crimes vnpunyshed. . . . Such like Terrors as these [described in Oedipus] requyreth this our present Age, wherin Vice hath chyefest place, and Vertue put to flyght: lyes as an abiect, languishynge in great extremytie. For the whiche cause, so muche the rather haue I suffred this my base trāslated Tragedie to be publyshed.[60]

fest in Burrant's preface to Cato (1545), in which the translator speaks of "the wittye, sage, yea, rather diuyne and heauenlye, then humayne and worldlye scyences of the antique Philosophers." He further declares that in his translation nothing is wanting "to the perfeccyon of Chrystes religyon, sauynge the hope and faith that a Chrysten manne oughte to haue in the bloude of Iesu Christ."

[58] Colyn, ibid. See also pp. 58-59, supra.

[59] "For almost all are covetous, all love gifts. There is no truth, no liberality, no knowledge of God. Men have broken forth to curse and to lie, and murder, and steal, and commit adultery. . . . The English indulge in pleasures, as if they were to die to morrow; while they build, as if they were to live always."—Bishop Parkhurst, Zurich Letters, April 28, 1562. With this statement compare Colyn's diseases of the mind (or spirit) "arrogance, superfluitie, ambition, Couetice, immesurable desyre of lyuinge, and . . . IGNORANCE . . . where she is, God is not duely honnored, vyce ys not eschued, nor any publique nor priuate action, or offyce, is rightfully & in order admynistred."—Op. cit.

[60] "To the Reader." For the value of the classics for the promotion of morality and religion, see further Hoby, p. 59, supra, Bavand, and Googe, op. cit.

With less feeling William Elderton indicates the relationship between the translation movement and the reformation,

> Philosophers learnings are ful of good warnings,
>   In memorye yet left to scoole vs,
> So bee ther contayned, in poietries fained,
>   Great documents to rate and rule vs;
>
> .   .   .   .   .
>
> Methinks that these pagons may counsel good Christians
>   With diligence to hear and mind them.[61]

Thus histories were issued because of the training in morals which they were thought to afford,[62] and the plays of Seneca were translated because of their power to arouse conscience. Similarly the *Satires* of Horace, who "was excellent good in his time, a muche zelous controller of sinne," were published, with some adaptation to make them the more pointed for the Elizabethans, in the same volume with the *Lamentations of Jeremiah*, the one writer to laugh at current evil and the other to weep over it.[63] Ovid, Apuleius, and Heliodorus were said to set forth pictorially, side by side, both vices and virtues in order to develop the moral judgment.[64] The *novelle* of Bandello and other renaissance writers of fiction[65] even had their place in the moral education of women.

It may seem strange that Puritans should thus sanction heathen and immoral literature, but it must be remem-

---

[61] *Collection of Seventy-nine Black Letter Ballads*, Joseph Lilly, editor, pp. 138, 140.

[62] Brend, *op. cit.*

[63] Drant, *Horace*, 1566 (*Jahrbuch der Deutschen Shakespeare Gesellschaft*, 47:48).

[64] See pp. 113-115, *infra*.

[65] Painter, *Palace of Pleasure* (Jacobs edition, p. 5); Fenton, *Certaine Tragicall Discourses* (Douglas edition, pp. 4, 5, 8). A satirical attitude toward women was pre-renaissance and pre-reformation. Contrast Barker's *Of the Nobility of Women*, cited p. 142, *infra*.

bered that the early Puritans were rationalists and realists, with strong tendencies toward individualism, and
sought to strengthen the moral fiber of the nation by edu-
cating the judgment and awakening the consciences of
individuals. They, accordingly, proposed to supplant the
impractically idealistic and authoritative view of medieval ethics with a realistic, analytical one, and believed
that individual morality was a necessary accompaniment
of the new individual freedom established by the revolution.

The inherent harmony between Protestantism and classicism which thus showed itself in a moral and religious
alignment is also revealed in a common prejudice against
medievalism in general. A word, according to contemporary usage, synonymous with "ignorance" was the term
"idleness";[66] and the power of the evil designated by it
to muddle and craze the whole nation is symbolically
presented in a reformation, humanistic morality play entitled, *The Longer Thou Liuest, the More Fool Thou Art*
(1559 or 1560).[67] Here "Idleness," "the parent of all
vice" is shown employing, among others of his assistants,

[66] The use of this term by various writers in the sixteenth century
may have been at times a mere convention, and often there is nothing
in the context to indicate what its connotation was, as, for example, in
Hawes, Berners (cited by Berdan, *Early Tudor Poetry*, pp. 370-371),
Miles Haggard (Collier, *op. cit.*, 2 : 137), Smyth (*Herodian*, Dedication),
Phaer (*Vergil*, Dedication), Golding (*Caesar*, Dedication), and Turberville (*Mantuan*, Dedication) ; but the discussions of "idleness" and "in-
dustry" by Elyot (*op. cit.*, 1 : 13; 3 : 23, 26, Par. 2) and the references by
the translators and their friends to themselves as "busy" men and to
their work as "painful" exercises and "trauayles" (Turberville, "Captious Sort of Sycophants," ll. 37-38; *ibid.*, verses in Fenton's *Certaine
Tragicall Discourses;* Sir John Conway, *ibid.;* commendatory verses in
Studley's *Agamemnon* and *Medea, passim;* Googe, *Zodiake of Lyfe,*
Dedication, 1565, Arber edition, p. 13; *et al; cf.* Elyot, *op. cit.*, 3 : 27,
end) give one the impression that the "eschewing of idleness" was a
renaissance shibboleth.

[67] *Jahrbuch der Deutschen Shakespeare Gesellschaft,* 36 : 1-64.

"Impietie," identified in the play with the philosophy of the schoolmen, "Ignorance," identified with medieval tradition, and "Wrath," symbolizing the deeds of violence and excesses sanctioned in medieval romance literature. These agents first render nugatory the instruction offered by characters symbolic of the humanists, and then cause their victim, the people, to be schooled in all the viciousness of the times. The immoral implications of the term "idleness,"[68] its close kinship to the term "ignorance," and the corrective value of the classics are here made evident. Similar conceptions of the baneful effect of idleness later appear in Lyly,[69] Nashe,[70] Stubbes,[71] and Lodge,[72] Nashe and Stubbes particularizing as to the evils which it produces: dicing, bowling (which begets gambling), gluttony, drunkenness, whoredom.

The translators also frequently used this word, characterizing those who opposed the new movement as "slothfull sluggerds,"[73] "drones,"[74] "doltes" and "idle lobs,"[75] men of "lumpish idle life"[76] and

curyous, fantasticall parsons, pryuey dyffamours of dylygent and vertuous laboure. who . . . ydely or with silence passe theyr tyme.[77]

[68] "Specially idlenes is an omission of al honest exercise."—Elyot, op. cit., 1:26. Cf. ibid., 1:12.

[69] Euphues (1579), (Croll and Clemens edition, p. 98).

[70] Pierce Pennilesse (1592), (McKerrow edition, 1:208-210).

[71] Anatomy of Abuses of England, Part I, "To the Reader," New Shakespeare Society, p. xi.

[72] "Idleness which hath beene the destruction of Sodome and Gomorrha." Catharos, fol. 25a.

[73] Nuce, p. 91, infra.

[74] Wilson, Demosthenes, Dedication.

[75] Whetstone, "A Remembraunce," Chalmers, English Poets, 2:460. These names appear in the text in the singular number. In this poem Whetstone is speaking of Gascoigne's troubles.

[76] Turberville, "Captious Sort of Sycophants," l. 55.

[77] Nicolls, Thucydides, Dedication (1550).

They declared themselves enemies of idleness, which they defined as the "Mother & nourissher of al vice,"[78] the "lothsome and horrible Monster,"[79] and the "mother of ignorance . . . nurse of aspiring and disloyall minds."[80, 81]

Condemnation of Medieval Literature

ONE result of this complete condemnation of all things medieval was that English literature inspired by the middle ages was considered by the Puritan classicists both enfeebling to the intellect and pernicious to sound morals. Medieval romances, but more especially the numerous ballads[82] produced during the period, constituted a menace to the progress of the renaissance and the reformation.

No doubt the cause that bookes of learnynge seme so hard is, because such and so greate a scull of amarouse Pamphlets haue so preoccupyed the eyes, and eares of men, that a multytude beleue ther is none other style, or phrase ells worthe gramercy. No bookes so ryfe or so frindly red, as be these bokes. . . . For good thyngs are hard, and euyl things are easye.[83]

[78] Golding, *Trogus*, "To the Reader."

"The Mystres of wanton appetites and portres of lustes gates."—*Institution of a Gentleman*. The writer recommends the reading of classical histories as a safeguard against idleness. *Cf.* Chaucer, "Persones Tale," Par. 57: Lawlesse lust . . . the Which aryseth and taketh hys begynning of Idlenesse."—Sanford, *Plutarch*, Dedication.

[79] Newton, *Cicero*, Dedication.

[80] Paulet, *Marquise of Idlenesse*, Collier, *op. cit.*, 2:133. William Paulet (1535?-1598), grandson of the Marquis of Winchester, was admitted to the Middle Temple in 1578.

[81] To many the term "idleness" was associated with monastic life. Ascham, *Scholemaster*, see pp. 79-80, *infra;* Green, *Short History of the English People*, p. 339. In other words, they held medieval influences responsible for most of the current abuses, whether in private life, church, or state.

[82] *Cf.* Crane, *Vogue of Guy of Warwick*, PMLA, 30, O. S.: 147.

[83] Drant, *Horace*, "To the Reader," 1567 (*Jahrbuch der Deutschen Gesellschaft*, 47: 53).

These "flim flams" and "gew gaws,"[84] "wanton allurements to leudnesse,"[85] "dongehyll matters"[86] filled the stationers' shops, they complain, and far outsold translations.[87] Even more than the content, the spirit of medieval literature offended the classical realists.

"If I shall compare it," Underdown says of his *Heliodorus*, "with other of its argument, I thinke none cometh neere it. Mort Darthur, Arthur of little Britaine, yea, and Amadis of Gaule etc. accompt violente murder, or murder for no cause, manhoode, and fornication and all vnlawfull luste, friendly love.[88]

William Parker, a member of Lincoln's Inn and one of Studley's friends, objected to the contemporary balladeers on the ground that, besides indulging in scurrilous attacks upon the men of the renaissance,[89] they were sordid in purpose and their work was debilitatingly paltry in its conceptions, verbose, loaded with stylistic ornamentation,[90] erotic, and generally vicious.[91] Medieval literature, moreover, was closely associated in the current thought with Roman Catholicism, for romances were reputed to have originated in monasteries[92] and ballads

[84] Drant, *Horace*, "To the Reader," 1567 (*Jahrbuch der Deutschen Gesellschaft*, 47:53).

[85] Underdown, *Heliodorus*, "To the Gentle Reader" (Whibley edition, p. 4).

[86] Henry Parker, Lord Morley, *Triumphes of Petrarcke*, 1553(?). "Robyn Hoode, or some other dongehyll matter," *op. cit.*, p. 4.

[87] Underdown, *ibid.*; *cf.* Lord Morley, *ibid.*

[88] Underdown, *ibid.*, p. 4. Possibly the difficulties which the translators had with the printers, referred to by Lord Morley, Heywood (*Thyestes*, Preface, de Vocht edition, pp. 104-105, ll. 337-350), and Drant reflect an antagonistic attitude toward the renaissance, on the part of the publishing profession.

[89] See pp. 90-92, *infra*.

[90] See pp. 70-71, *supra*.

[91] Verses in Studley's *Agamemnon* (Spearing edition, pp. 14-15, ll. 310-325).

[92] "In our forfathers tyme, when Papistrie, as a standyng poole, couered and ouerflowed all England, fewe bookes were read in our tong, sauing certaine bookes Cheualrie, as they sayd, for pastime and pleasure, which, as some say, were made in Monasteries, by idle Monkes, or wan-

were frequently distributed from the same peddlers' bags as the polemics emanating from the English Catholics gathered at Louvain.[93, 94] Hence, the translators made war upon the popular writers of the time, who returned the charge.[95]

By and large the new party had adopted the comprehensive program of destroying everything medieval. Having cut themselves away from institutions of the past as a means of political, social, and religious support, they sought in increased knowledge and the exercise of individual judgment the force which would insure the realm

ton Chanons: as for example Morte Arthure, the whole pleasure of which booke standeth in two speciall poyntes, in their open mans slaughter and bold bawdrye."—Ascham, *Scholemaster* (Arber edition, p. 80).

A score of years later (1512) Nashe voiced the continued classical protest against romantic literature. The writers were obscurantists, persons "voide of all knowledge . . . that obtrude themselues vnto vs, as the Authors of eloquence and fountains of our finer phrases, when as they sette before vs nought but a confused masse of wordes without matter." —*Works* (McKerrow edition, 1 : 10).

Like Nicolls (p. 70, *supra*, note 44) he complains of the damage done by them to historical knowledge, calling romances and popular literature, "Histories of antiquitie . . . belyed" (McKerrow, *ibid.*) and like Ascham charges them with giving support to lust and vice. He also reasserts the monastic origin of romances.

"What els I pray you doe these bable bookmungers endeuor, but to repaire the ruinous wals of Venus Court, to restore to the worlde that forgotten Legendary licence of lying, to imitate a fresh the fantasticall dreames of those exiled Abbie-lubbers, from whose idle pens proceeded those worne out impressions of the feyned no where acts, of Arthur of the rounde table, Arthur of litle Brittaine, Sir Tristam, Hewon of Burdeaux, the Squire of low degree, the foure sons of Amon, with infinite others."—*Ibid.*, 1 : 11.

Hake, *Newes out of Powles Churchyarde* (Satire 6, ll. 4, 8, 11, 162 ff., 268-274), contains reference to slanders, taunts, jests, and filthy stories told in the Papists' Walk, St. Paul's.

[93] *A Collection of Seventy-nine Black Letter Ballads*, Joseph Lilly, editor, p. 207.

[94] In 1589 Nashe was still objecting to the cheap, medieval fiction. "The ouerseeing of that *sublime dicendi genus*, which walkes abroade for wast paper in each seruing-mans pocket, and the otherwhile perusing of our Gothamists barbarisme."—*Works* (McKerrow edition, 3 : 314).

[95] See pp. 113, 115, *infra.*

from disturbance both from within and from without, and in the appeal to conscience they trusted for the continued success of the reformation, the movement with which every other phase of the new movement was involved.

CHAPTER V

RECEPTION AND OPPOSITION

The Translators' Public

MUCH concerning the translators' reading public can be gleaned from the number of editions issued and from contemporary statements. Twelve of the fifty or sixty translations from the classics put out between the years 1557 and 1572, inclusive, went through more than one edition, two of them appearing three times. Four books, published too late to register their popularity in the period selected, were reissued within the next eight years. Ovid had four translators; Horace, three; Vergil, Trogus Pompeius, and Heliodorus each two.[1] Seven parts of Cicero and two of Epictetus appeared. Of the translations of earlier reigns, one was republished three times, three, twice, and four, once. Though a complaint made by a printer to Drant to the effect that translations were not so profitable as current fiction[2] was intended as an insinuation that the demand

---

[1] Golding published four books of the *Metamorphoses* in 1565 and the completed book in 1567; selections from the same work were translated by Howell in 1560, Peend in 1565, and Hubbard in 1569. Evans in 1564/5 and Drant in 1566 translated Horace's *Satires*. Drant in 1567 and an anonymous writer in 1566/7 did the *Epistles*. In 1557 appeared Surrey's *Aeneid*, Book II new and Book IV reissued, in 1558 Phaer's seven books, and in 1562 his nine and a half. *Trogus Pompeius* (a selection) was translated by Norton in [1560?] and by Golding (entire) in 1564. A portion of *Heliodorus* was executed by Sanford in 1567 and the whole of it by Underdown in 1568/9. For reissues of earlier translations, see p. 19 n., *supra*.

[2] *Horace*, "To the Reader," 1567, *op. cit.*, 47:53.

for the former was small, these figures would indicate that the translators' constituency was at least sizable.

It comprised, we are told, both the learned and the un-learned, *i.e.*, those who could read Latin and those who could not. To the former, so far as they were scholars and friends, the translators looked for correction, just ap-praisal, and sympathetic appreciation.[3] Many of these cer-tainly were of the nobility. On the other hand, the inter-est of the unlearned was even more sought after.

Because I could not mysdoubt, but the learned had already tried it; to thintente, that the vnlearned also, might haue some fruicion thereof.[4]

Yet I so reposed my hope in thee, that it gaue me corage to trās-late this one Tragedie more of SENECA, for the pleasure of the learned, and the profyte of the vnlearned by the readynge of it in theyr natyue language.[5]

And therefore to returne to Demosthenes, I saye, he is to be read of yong and olde, of learned and vnlearned, of wyse, and vnwyse, for that he hath in hym to serue all mens turnes whatsoeuer.[6]

The unthinking masses were too hopelessly bound by tradition and prejudice to be susceptible of education,

---

[3] "Submitting it to the freindly correction of the learned."—Studley, *Agamemnon*, Preface (Spearing edition, p. 23).

"Both Cambridge and Oxford men, haue giuen me their helping hands."—Wilson, *Demosthenes*, Preface, fol. 10a.

"Vnto the Iudgement of the wyse and learned, I
Submit my paynes (to pleasure thē) perswaded thorowlye:
That with aduisement they will speake, and reason ryght
Shall rule theyr tongues. . . .

.   .   .   .   .

That learned men alowe these same, it shall to me
Suffyse."

—Peend, *Mendozza*, "To the Reader."
Cf. Turberville, *Rayling Route* (Chalmers, *English Poets*, 2:584).

[4] Dolman, *op. cit.*, Dedication. *Cf.* Phaer, *Aeneid* (1558), "To Good Readers."

[5] Studley, *Medea*, Preface (Spearing edition, p. 125).

[6] Wilson, *Demosthenes*, Preface, fol. 9b.

and did not come into the translators' reckoning. But many of Elizabeth's nobles had but recently been raised to the titled class, and the rapid growth of the national wealth had produced an influential bourgeoisie hardly to be distinguished from the nobility.[7] Great numbers of both of these groups had no skill in reading the classics in the original, yet intellectually they were among the most vigorous part of the nation. To them Dolman appealed directly.

Besydes the raskall multitude, and the learned sages, there is a meane [*i.e.*, intermediate] sort of men: which although they be not learned, yet, by the quicknes of their wits, can conceiue al such poyntes of arte, as nature could giue. To those, I saye, there is nothing in this book to darke.[8]

The chief care of the new order, then, was to acquaint this virile central group with the principles of the renaissance, for, though the simon-pure reactionaries could not be affected, by securing the adherence of this substantial class of open-minded people the ruling minority might hope to retain the power.

Opposition to Translation

YET the translators' work was not universally well received, for Dolman says also of the translators' critics,

Though I craue no prayse at thy handes . . . yet, I may be bold, to desire so much of the, as Apelles comaunded of the foolishe shoomaker, to performe. . . . Shewynge thereby, that no man oughte to talke farther, then his skill will beare him.[9]

[7] Phaer addressed "the nobilitie, gentlemen and Ladies, that studie not Latine." *Op. cit.* It might be concluded also from the nature of the *Courtier* that those who besought Hoby to translate it were many of them noble. See p. 38, *supra.*

[8] *Op. cit.,* Preface.

[9] *Op. cit.,* Preface. For the allusion see p. 90 n., *infra.*

Moreover, the opposition to liberal influences was active and violent, for many translators refer to it much more explicitly. In fact, hardly any other one topic receives the amount of attention in the dedications and prefaces that the opposition to the translation of the classics does, and the protection of patrons is repeatedly besought to counteract it.[10] Neville thus addresses Dr. Wotton, a member of the Queen's Privy Council,

So am I driuen humbly to requyre your strong ayde, & assured Defence against the sclaunderous assaults of such malicious mouths.[11]

Similar words are employed by others:

Therefore . . . beseching your Lordship to take vpon you the tuicion of so weake a Fortresse, whom w^tout your trustie aide, the parlous force of yll tonges might soone ouerthrow. . . . I cease at this instant to trouble you.[12]

Assuring your self, that in defending and shrowdinge them against the poysoned and sclaunderous infamyes of serpentine Sicophantes, and the cancred assaultes of malicious tongues, whiche feede on no other repast but spightful disdaine and hellishe rancoure, your L shal do a thing (vnlesse I be much deceyued) greatly sounding to the generositie of youre noble hart and highe estate.[13]

[10] Such persistent and savage opposition can be accounted for only on the basis of some such explanation of the translators' purposes and relations as is made in the present volume. Conversely, its existence corroborates the evidence set forth in a previous chapter of an alliance between the translators and the Protestant leaders of the nation.

[11] *Oedipus*, Dedication.

[12] Studley, *Medea*, Dedication to the Earl of Bedford, 1566 (Spearing edition, p. 124).

[13] Newton, *Cicero*, Dedication to the Marquis of Winchester, 1569.

"If the wisdome that God at these yeres in your highnes hath planted, had not seemde to me a strong defence against all byt of shameles arrogāce (reproche wherof flong with disdainfull wordes from ireful tōgues, as adders stinges should strike me) . . . I would not haue incurred so daungerous note of presumption, in attempting a subiect to hys princesse."—Heywood, *Troas*, Dedication to the Queen, 1559 (de Vocht edition, pp. 3, 4).

Identification of the Translators' Opponents

THIS is strong language, but if, as we have attempted to show, the translators and the liberal party were aligned against the medieval reactionaries in state, church, and life, some evidence of the resistance of the latter, more than that the translators' writings were subjected to caustic and violent criticism, should be forthcoming.[14] Some

"But wheras no mã lyues so vpryghtly, whom slaundring toonges leaue vndyffamed: I referre my self to the Iudgement of yᵉ wysest, lytle esteaming the preiudicall mouthes of suche carping Marchauntes, whiche suffre no mennes doynges almoste to scape vndefyled."—Neville, *Oedipus*, Preface, 1563.

"To endaunger my selfe in gyuynge them [the *Eglogs*] to lyght, to the disdaynfull doome of any offended mynde."—*Eglogs*, Dedication to William Lovelace, Esq., 1563 (Arber edition, p. 24).

"The fauorable accepting of my simple trauayles lately dedicated vnto your honor, hath so much boldened and thorowelye encouraged me, that mawgre the despite of most reprochfull tongs, I haue not feared to finish the course of my long pretended race: with no lesse profite as I trust, vnto a number, than paynefull trauayle vnto my selfe."—Googe, *Zodiake of Lyfe*, Dedication to Cecil, 1565 (Arber edition of *Eglogs*, p. 13).

"First in yᵗ I cõsidered your honours aucthor[it]ie, wisedome, & learning, (takyng the tuicion of it vpon you) might be a terrour, and abashment, to such slaunderous tongs, who by my symple and slender skill, eyther in this or any other lyke facultie, myght take courage rather of maliciousnes (then of ryght) to reprehend my doings."—Studley, *Agamemnon*, Dedication to Cecil, 1566 (Spearing edition, pp. 19-20).

"I . . . desired, as the common custome is, some Patron, that myght both bring aucthoritye to thys my little Booke, and also, if neede should be, defend it from the bitter taunts of enuious tongs."—Nuce, *Octavia*, Dedication to Leicester, 1566.

"I may be thought to haue attempted a bold enterprise to take vpon me (being yet in my nonage) such a work as few or none have done at like yeares, also knowing the daunger thereof, which is the hasardyng of my good name."—Watson, *Polybius*, 1569, "To the Reader."

"And thus hauing done my voluntarie taske, I desire none other thankes, for all my labor and traueyle herein, but your fauourable defence against certaine, that will doe nothing themselues, and yet will finde fault with all thinges."—Wilson, *Demosthenes*, Dedication to Cecil, 1570. Fol. 6b.

[14] See p. 85, *supra*.

of the terms applied by the translators to their opponents
were "Momus," "sycophant," and "Zoilus," to which
were commonly attached one or more of the epithets
"curious," "spiteful," "envious," "carping," "scornful,"
"rancorous," "poisoned," and "idle."[15] Of the first of
these, "Momus," the current definition was, "a curious
carper"; and of "sycophant," "he that falsely accuseth
an innocent," also, "a bearer of tales, or a cōplainer."[16]
But more illuminating is Erasmus' definition of "Zoilus,"

*Zoili audax quidem, sed parum felix mordacitas prouerbio locum
fecit, ut uulgo Zoili uocētur, alienarum laudum obtrectatores, &
alienorū laborum reprehensores. Hic Zoilus sophista quispiam
fuit, hoc facinore potissimum nobilitatus, q, Homerum poetarum
omnium principem ausus est, libris in eum scriptis incessere . . .
sic enim appellantur nobilium autorum castigatores.*[17]

[15] Child (*Cambridge History of English Literature*, 1909, 3 : 187)
has made the very casual comment concerning Turberville's and Roy-
den's use of the term "sycophant" that these two poets refer to "critics."
Tupper (*J.E.G.P.*, 16 : 551-572) has listed various passages occurring
in the dedications and prefaces of English books from the twelfth
to the eighteenth century, in which the word "envy" is found. His
conclusion, however, that the employment of the term is a mere
convention, can hardly stand, for, first, his method of promiscuous
collection over so long a period, without reference to historical data,
tends to obliterate whatever significance there might be; second, his
study of a single word furnishes insufficient materials for a broad
generalization; and, third, his omission of some important passages tends
to invalidate his thesis. A prologue which apparently did not come to
Tupper's notice contains the following statement:
"Heare I will speake nothing of the enuious that thinkethe it not de-
cent to wryte any liberall arte in the vulgar tongue, but would haue
all thinges kept close eyther in the Hebrewe, Greke or Latyn tongues.
I knowe what greate hurte hath come to the Church of God by the defense of this mischeuous opiniō." Roll, *Logicke*, "Epistle to the Reader,"
1574.

[16] Cooper, *Bibliotheca Eliotae*, 1552. Zoilus was a fourth century
(B.C.) grammarian, who assailed Homer, and whose name in consequence became a synonym for a captious and malignant critic. He
"found fault with him for introducing fabulous and incredible stories
in his poems."—*Smith's Classical Dictionary*.

[17] *Adagia*, 1530. Cf. Ovid, *Remedio Amoris*, ll. 365-366; Martial,
11 : 37 : 1, *et al*.

Likewise Cooper defines Zoilus as

a poete, whiche enuied Homerus: and therfore the enuiers of well lerned men are called Zoili.[18]

In other words, "Zoilus" was a synonym for "anti-humanist," and the early use of the word in that sense accounts for the observation of Heywood, a student of Erasmus' writings,[19] that the detractors of the translators

are long syns sproong vp of Zoylus Bloode.[20]

In the sense of "obscurantist" "Zoilus" continued to be employed throughout the century and later.[21]

But it was a specific rather than a general term; and the Zoili's tenets and principles have been stated with considerable fulness by Bale. From him it is to be learned that these individuals were enemies to Protestantism; university men, adept in scholastic philosophy; medieval stylists; readers of the ancient authors that were in vogue during the middle ages, Aristotle and Vergil, but not of the renaissance favorites, Plato and Cicero:

The other is Momus or Zoilus, yes, rather one which playeth both parts under the cloak of a Christian. This cruel carper and malicious quarreller leaveth no man's work unrebuked, minister it never so much godliness. But like as rust, moths, maggots, cankers, caterpillars, with other vile vermin, corrupteth all that is to the use of man; so doth this enemy, to destroy both name and work, only for the advancement of his own precious person.

His working tools are such unsavoury sophisms, problems, elenches, corrolaries, quiddities, subtilties, second intentions, intrinsical moods, with other prodigious sorceries, whom he sometime sucked out of his mother's breasts, the university. These hath he not yet all, as unsavoury morsels, evomited for Christ, de-

[18] *Op. cit.*
[19] *Hercules Furens*, Dedication (de Vocht edition, p. 198).
[20] *Thyestes*, Preface, l. 222 (de Vocht edition, p. 100).
[21] See p. 100 n., *infra*.

fining rather with Aristotle than with Paul in his daily disputations. Of this royal rabbi is Peter judged a fool, and John an unlearned idiot. Yet shall his reader find small learning at his hand, unless he take an heap of barbarous terms, and unsewed together sentences, for matters of excellent learning. . . .

But Momus hath not yet done away with the mad mists of his mocking, nor yet the dark dregs of his sophistry, which both are a great blemishing unto his eye-sight. The wisdom of Plato, Homer, and Cicero, availeth nothing in this. Aristotle and Virgil, if they were alive, could herein do little or nothing. Inestimably more maketh the poor fishers' learning to the understanding of these mysteries, than the proud painted eloquence or far fet reasons of the philosophers.[22]

The particularity and the acrimonious character of the utterances of the translators who were in closest touch with Oxford and Cambridge—Heywood, Dolman, Phaer, Drant, Nuce, Studley (whose friends at his request[23] contributed sharply satirical verses to his volume of Seneca's plays), Googe, and Turberville,[24] are further evidence that the universities were an important source of the opposition to the translation movement. Phaer and Dolman indeed explicitly so state.

Trustyng that you my right worshipfull maisters, & studentes of vniuersities, and such as be teachers of childern and reders of this auctour in latyn, will not be to muche offended, though euery verse answere not to your expectation.[25]

Knowynge, that if such, as haue greater knoweledge, to set forthe thinges more exactlye, should heare my plainenesse not ouermuche discommended; they then, should be much more prouoked, wyth hope of the meruaylous fame, that their doings should deserue if

[22] *Works* (Parker Society, pp. 381, 515), *The Image of Both Churches*, Prefaces, Pts. 2 and 3. One of Bale's English dramatic works was entitled *Ergo Momus & Zoilus* (*Scriptorum illustrium Britanniae Catalogus*).

[23] Nuce, verses prefixed to the *Agamemnon*, l. 51 (Spearing edition, p. 5).

[24] See biographical data, pp. 141 ff., *infra*.

[25] *Aeneid*, Preface.

they listed, to employe some paynes, in attempting the like. Of the whych, as I know there is a great number (in both vniuersities inespecially) so I woulde wyshe, that eyther they ceassyng any longer, to enuie knowledge to our Englyshe tounge, would staine the same, with better: or els, that they woulde not disdaine to forde their fauourable wordes, to suche, as expresse their good will in the same: althoughe not so well as it might be, yet as theyr eloquence will permit them.[26]

Yet had the academicians been the only opponents with whom the translators had had to contend, the whole controversy might have been little more than a tempest in a tea-pot. Another class of the Zoili to whom reference is continually being made,[27] appear to have been even more numerous.

That Red heard, black mouthd, squint eyed wretche / hath cowched euery wheare,
Jn corner close Jmpe of his / that sitts to see and heare
What eche man dothe, and eche man blames, / nor onse we may him see
Come face to face, but we once gone / then stoutly stepps out hee:
And all he carpes that there he fyndes / ere halfe he reade to ende,

[26] *Op. cit.*, Preface.

[27] The distinction between learned and unlearned Zoili was made by at least four of the translators in passages scattered in point of time throughout the period of this study: Googe, 1560, see *infra*; Dolman, 1561, *op. cit.*, Preface; Drant, 1567, *Horace*, "To the Reader"; and Gascoigne, 1575, "To al Young Gentlemen," Chalmers, *English Poets*, 2: 470.

"The learned wyttes I heare requyre with rigour not to iudge.
The common sort I noughte esteme vnskilful though they grudge.
Nor few of them can hold theyr peace but finde them selues a doe,
In vewing workes as he that sought, to mende Apelles shoe."
—Googe, *Zodiake of Lyfe*, "The book to the reader" (Arber edition of the *Eglogs*, p. 8).

Dolman, *op. cit.*, and Golding, *Caesar*, make similar reference to the critic of Apelles. The story originated from Pliny, *Historia Naturalis*, 25: 10, who tells how a common man, having successfully criticized the shoe in Apelles' picture of Venus, went on to offer further objections and was reproved by the painter for so doing.

And what he vnderstandes not, blames, / though nought he can
amende.[28]

Omnipresent, ignorant, and particularly voluble, without
honesty or powers of comprehension, these actively en-
deavored to discourage the translators through "spight,
suspect, and care"[29] with no better motives for their "captious," "carping" assaults than "envy,"[30] "rancour,"[31] and
love of slander.[32]

I know this painfull wight / can not hys carpers want,
Whych often tymes discorage men, / and make such studyes
skant.   .   .   .   .

Such Emules, & such fyendly freaks, / if E thou take away,
Playn Mules they be, yᵗ mump & mow, / and nothyng els can
say,
Who if in ranckours, poysoned sincke, / they lurke and wallow
styll,
Nor yet with cancred venome bolne, / do leaue theyr waspysh
will,
But slothfull sluggerds still vpbraid, / that paynfull heads
deuyse,
And with their tryple forked tongs, / anoy thys enterpryse
Discorage him from other worke, / and further fruytes of wit,
And other toward paynes dysgrace, / if they such poyson spit.[33]

28 Heywood, *Thyestes*, Preface, ll. 223-234 (de Vocht edition, pp.
100-101). *Cf.* Martial, 12:54. See also verses prefixed to Studley's *Agamemnon*, by W. R., ll. 224-226 (Spearing edition, p. 11); by T. B., ll.
392-393 (*ibid.*, p. 18); Turberville, *Heroycall Epistles*, "Captious Sort
of Sycophants," ll. 61-66.
29 Whetstone, "A Remembraunce of a Wel Imployed Life," l. 102
(Chalmers, *English Poets*, 2:460).
30 Verses prefixed to Studley's *Agamemnon*, by Nuce, ll. 1-6 (Spearing
edition, p. 3); by W. R., l. 239 (*ibid.*, p. 10); by Peend, ll. 293-294 (*ibid.*,
p. 14); verses prefixed to Studley's *Medea*, by W. P., ll. 121-123 (*ibid.*,
p. 127); Turberville, "Captious Sort," ll. 40-48; Whetstone, *op. cit.*, ll.
97-114.
31 Nuce, *infra*.
32 See p. 85 and note, *supra;* Nuce, *ibid.*, l. 161.
33 Nuce, *ibid.*, ll. 59-60, 71-82.

"To whet his poysoned-räckling teth, I cast the curre a bone:
  Lest that hee seeke to byte my name behynde my backe,
  To saye that here his verse is lame, or here good sense doth lacke.

> Pluck out that bloudie Faurton (Discard thou)
> Wherewith thou full many a skirmish made
> And scocht the braines of many a learned brow.[34]

Slothful, vile-mouthed "dolts,"[35] who in their writings
did not hesitate from "learned authors" to "filch terms to
paint a prattling tung"[36] and to "gape for glorious renoume,"[37] they were thoroughly unscrupulous.

> But as thou ert in all thy other deedes
> Deseruing no beliefe·or trust at all;
> Likewise what from thy vile Jawes proceedes
> Is loathsome lie fowle fitton, bitter Gall.[38]

Accordingly, the whole new literary movement had to be
carried on in the face of a maximum of annoyance from
these blockading pirates.

> For I ofte times haue heard the vyle despysed sorte
> Blynd ignorantes, of worthie bokes to make such rashe reporte:
> That when in order good, they could not read the same,
> They doubted not by slaūderous wordes the aucthors to defame.
>
> · · · ·
>
> Theyr brutische braynes vnfit to iudge of melodye,
> Their blinded wittes, & sences stopt do vnto them denie
> The vse of reason so: that monsters ryght they be,
> Despised dregges of men, to them in shape alone agree
> Or els ryght πανφαγοι and currysh whelpes they weare,
> Their iudgements I do now despise: theyr rage I do not feare."
>
> —Peend, *Mendozza*, "To the Reader."

[34] Turberville, "Rayling Route," ll. 32-34.

[35] Whetstone, *op. cit.*, l. 129.

[36] *Ibid.*, ll. 103-114.

[37] W. Parker, verses prefixed to Studley's *Agamemnon*, l. 319 (*op. cit.*, p. 15).

[38] Turberville, "Rayling Route," ll. 55-58; see also *ibid.*, "Captious Sort," ll. 49-52. "But let those curious Knightes cast an eye to home, and looke well about, whether they themselues are blameless, or as well worthie reproche as others."—*Ibid.*, *Epitaphes, Epigrams, Songes, and Sonets*, "To the Reader"; Nuce, *op. cit.*, ll. 70-190; "their corrupt consciences gauled with the discoverie of their monstrous deceites."—Whetstone, *Rock of Regard*, General Advertisement; Neville, Googe's *Eglogs*, ll. 13-56 (Arber edition, pp. 21-22). "I meane curyous, fantasticall parsons, pryuey dyffamours of dylygent and vertuous laboure, who, though they themself to theyr reproche do ydely or with silence passe theyr tyme, be yet greuously pynched wyth enuye that other shulde trauayle to vtter theyr talente to the commodytie of many, therby to proffet."—Nicolls, *Thucydides,· Dedication, 1550.

Who sekes to shun ye shattring sails of mighty Momus mast,
Must not attempt ye sugred seas, where muses ancour cast.
For Momus there doth ryde at flote, with scornefull tonges
    yfraght:
With cancred cracks of wrathfull words he keeps the passage
    strayght.
That none without disdaine may passe where muses nauie lies,
But straight on them with ireful mode the scornful God he flies.
Since none may scape, I am not he, that can my self assure:
Through surging seas of depe disdaine my passage to procure.
But am content for to receiue reproche at Momus hand:
Syth none there is, that may the nose of Rhynocere withstand.[39]

Through the agency of this unwashed company, the propaganda against the new movement in all its phases, political, ecclesiastical, and cultural, was carried on; and against them and their university trained instigators the translators begged their patrons for protection.

The "unlearned" Zoili were perhaps Papists who still maintained a status in the country; undoubtedly they were those conforming clergy whose reactionary influence over the general public naturally continued to be very great.

Those cackelinge pyes, that vse to prate / so much agaynst hu-
    manitye,
Are commonlye the lewdest dawes, / and skillesse in diuinity.[40]

But many of them were laymen, the writers of broadsides, who constituted Philistine Grub Street.[41]

[39] Googe, *Zodiake of Lyfe*, "The booke to the reader," 1560. *Op. cit.*, p. 7.

[40] Drant, *Horace, op. cit.*, p. 57.

[41] The classification employed is that of Hake, *Newes out of Powles Churchyarde* (1568?), "The Author to the Carping and scornefull Sicophant." His names for the three classes are Papists, Janus-jacks, and neutrals. For an estimate of the number of Papist priests still in England during the period, see Pollen, *English Catholics in the Reign of Elizabeth*, pp. 39-41. *Cf.* also Hake, *ibid.*, 6:ll. 209-297.

And last of all, I turne my tale to thee,
Thou *Nunquam sanus* vyle reprochfull mate,
And carping carelesse cankerd churle, whom hee
That writes eche where, reproues with worthy hate,
For that thou belkst with belly bursten paunch,
Gainst them that haps from ydle shoare to launch.[42]

All these, scholars, Papists, conforming clergy who
were unsympathetic with Protestantism and the new order in the state, and pamphleteers, were bent upon maintaining the popular prejudice in favor of Romanism, the
old learning, and the Spanish alliance. Among them even
rebellion and sedition found voice. Interesting evidence
of this fact appears in Securis' *Almanac* for 1569, the
momentous year when the Rebels of the North made
their stand and a time when the crisis with Spain was cul-
minating. On the title page of this household publication
appears the motto *"Non ostento sed ostendo propter
zoilos,"* and in the prognostication under the heading,
"Of peace and warre" occurs the prediction,

He [*i.e.,* Mars] sygnifieth also a multitude of hypocryts, yᵉ which
shal appeare outwardly clothed with Lamme skynnes, but in-
wardly are rauenyng wolfes,

a common characterization of the reactionary clergy. By
a curious coincidence a set of verses translated from Re-
giomontanus and placed at the beginning of the prognostication foretells the end of the world in 1588, the year
of the Spanish Armada.[43]

[42] Hake, *ibid.* Collier (*Bibliographical and Critical Account*) recog-
nizes the persons here described as the pamphleteers of the day. *Cf.*
W. Parker's reference to them (verses in Studley's *Agamemnon, op. cit.,*
p. 14). Since no example of the Zoili's writings against the translators
has been discovered, it is possible that much of their work was circu-
lated in manuscript.

[43] The writer of a manuscript note in the British Museum copy and
Bosanquet, *English Printed Almanacs and Prognostications,* p. 112, refer
to this as a definite prediction of the coming of the Armada.

Persecutions of the Translators

SINCE translating had become a vital issue in the political and religious turmoils of the nation, it is not difficult to understand the need of strong patronage. In Mary's time, Cheke, who had been the pillar of liberal influence, was the object of direct attack;[44] Grimald, who had been the humanist leader at Oxford, was induced to recant his Protestant views and to betray his associates to death; Cooper and Carre, as has been said, sought refuge in the practice of medicine;[45] and many were under the necessity of looking for safety abroad. Though many of these men suffered ostensibly for the sake of their religion, in that period Protestantism and the renaissance, as has been shown,[46] were inextricably intertwined. Wilson, for example, though he has been said to have suffered in the Roman Inquisition for his opposition to Cardinal Pole,[47] if his own statement is to be relied upon, fell into this persecution on account of his *Arte of Logic* and his *Arte of Rhetorique*.[48] Hoby's *Courtier*, which was ready for print probably in 1556, the date of the dedication, was withheld because of the opposition,[49] and the publication of the *Mirror for Magistrates*, to which the translators and their colleagues at the inns of court were the principal contributors, was interrupted by the order of Bishop Gardiner.[50]

At the beginning of Elizabeth's reign, since the opposition to Protestantism and the renaissance was held in

[44] See p. 10 n., *supra; cf.* also pp. 11-12, *supra.*
[45] See pp. 30-31, *supra.*
[46] See pp. 11-12, *supra.*
[47] DNB.
[48] *Arte of Rhetorique*, 1561, "Prologue," 1560. Paragraph 3.
[49] "Printer to the Reader" (Tudor Translations, p. 3).
[50] See p. 63, *supra.*

leash by the government, the danger to the translators of personal assault was slight. Still other annoyances awaited them, particularly slander and damaging reports,[51] which required the intervention of influential patrons. In our day of comparative safety, protection from envious tongues may seem a social rather than a civil desideratum, but in a century when rumor might even send one to the Tower, they were not to be disregarded.

But some concrete instances of the personal risks the translators ran and of the machinations of the Zoili against them are pertinent. After the lapse of nearly four centuries, it is really quite remarkable that one, and possibly, two cases of the sly persecution that went on are preserved. The first concerns the difficulties of Turberville. Turberville's apparently long-continued troubles are not completely understood, but they would seem to have been due to his activity in the liberal movement. They evidently began in 1567 or before, for in the *Heroycall Epistles* the poet forecasts that in consequence of his translating Ovid he will "feele the force of enuious Hate."[52] Subsequently, in the same year, he reports that his surmise has been correct, and again he anticipates that his own poems will be misconstrued into slander,[53] by which he may mean anything up to treason. According to Rollins' chronology of Turberville's career,[54] shortly afterwards, coincidentally with the period when the reactionaries were conducting military operations against the government[55] and expected assistance from Spain, he

[51] See p. 85 and note, *supra*.
[52] "The Translator to the Captious Sort of Sycophantes," l. 44.
[53] "To the Rayling Route of Sycophantes," in *Epitaphes, Epigrams, Songes, and Sonets* (Chalmers, *English Poets*, 2:583), ll. 43-47.
[54] *Modern Philology*, 15:528.
[55] Since Rollins' date is only approximate, a slight discrepancy is negligible.

made his attempt at translating Lucan to counteract seditious tendencies in the nation; and for so doing he was "mislikte."[56] The specific character of the "late troubles" which, he says, brought his work on Lucan to an end, is disclosed in an order issued by the Privy Council[57] calling for an investigation of the appointments of Hugh Bamfield (Turberville's uncle, to whom the poet had dedicated his translation of Mantuan, 1567) and Turberville, to captaincies in the army. Besides lack of experience in military affairs, the alleged charge against them was incompetence, the former on account of age, and the latter on account of devotion "to his boke and studie."[58] This chain of persecutions constitutes a concrete instance of the sort of annoyances against which the translators sought protection. Turberville had chosen patrons who were perhaps not the strongest, the Earl of Warwick, the most distinguished among them, not being admitted to the Privy Council till 1573, so that the agents of the old régime dared to molest the poet.[58a]

Gascoigne would seem to have been another victim of the Zoili. Whatever may be thought of Whetstone's "Remembraunce of a Wel Imployed life" as biography, its statement that Gascoigne was harassed by individuals, some of whom at least, from the account given of them, were among the pamphleteers, may not be neglected. While no attempt is to be made to fill up the lacunae in our knowledge of Gascoigne's career, certain fairly well

[56] See p. 51, *supra*.

[57] *Modern Philology, ibid.*

[58] The charges, of course, may have been justified, but in the light of all the circumstances they sound specious. Turberville at the time was about thirty years old and had but recently (1569) returned from Russia, where he had served as secretary to Sir Thomas Randolph, a Protestant of pronounced views.

[58a] Note might be made also of the Earl's continued ill health.

attested events of 1572 are of exceedingly great interest in the present connection. In that year, *A Hundreth sundrie Flowers*, the author's collected works, were issued through the agency of one H. W. and one G. T.—in all probability, the author's friend, George Turberville, whose persecutions by the Zoili have just been recounted. That these works were objects of attack is shown in the second edition, published in 1575, by the contribution of commendatory verses from numerous friends who insisted upon the worth and moral decency of the contents of the book and by two addresses of the author, who, besides reiterating the sentiments of his supporters with reference to the serious moral purpose of his poetry, protested that he had suffered an injustice since his poetry on the occasion of its first publication had "beene doubtfully construed, and (therefore) scandalous."[59] In spite of awkward phrasing, Gascoigne's meaning here is sufficiently clear, especially since a few pages later he vigorously disavows a charge that the "Adventures of Maister F.I." —a constituent part of his volume—had been "written to the scandalizing of some worthie personages, whom" those making the allegation "would seeme therby to know."[60] So far, then, as can be judged from Gascoigne's and Turberville's accounts of their experiences, these two

[59] Hazlitt edition, p. 1.

[60] *Ibid.*, p. 5. The question whether Gascoigne was the author of the "Adventures of Maister F.I." is not pertinent to the case, since according to the document under consideration, *To the reverende Diuines*, Gascoigne's authorship was assumed by his accusers and was not denied by the poet. (For the most recent discussion of the subject of the authorship, see Ward's edition of *A Hundreth sundrie Flowers*, which has appeared while the present volume has been going through the press.) In the *Review of English Studies*, 2:5:32 ff., Ward gives new dates for the publication of Gascoigne's works: 1573 for *A Hundreth sundrie Flowers* and 1576 for *Posies*, a reissue of the foregoing.

translators would seem to have suffered in much the same manner at the hands of the Zoili, for the part they took in the new literary movement.

Moreover, the attack upon Gascoigne likewise appears to have transcended mere words. In the early part of the year in which the works were first published he had been elected to Parliament from Midhurst, Sussex; in May a petition was presented to the Privy Council contesting his fitness for the office. Of the items of the brief offered, little can be said in reply to that alleging impecuniousness, for Gascoigne is known to have been a spendthrift. Of the accusation of manslaughter, no profitable discussion seems possible. But in the remaining charges the familiar methods of the Zoili are discernible. If a spy, as was said, like Churchyard,[61] he may have had occasion during the late period of rebellion to inform upon Papist plotters or suspects; and atheism, godlessness, and rhyming, as will be shown, were precisely the charges brought against other translators. Finally, that he was "a deuiser of slaunderous pasquilles againste diuerse personnes of great callinge," an accusation corresponding to that brought against Turberville, is in part certainly accounted for by the misconstruction put upon *A Hundreth sundrie Flowers*. Gascoigne, it should be observed, was even more defenseless than Turberville had been, in that he had brought out his works without any patronage whatsoever.

Hints of other annoyances to which the translators may have been subjected are too vague to receive any prolonged attention, but the number who express a fear of slanderous tongues[62] and the fervency of Studley's large

---

[61] *Chips concerning Scotland*, Letter to Cecil.
[62] See p. 85 and note, *supra*.

group of friends in his behalf when he published the *Aga-memnon* and the *Medea*[63] are sufficiently suggestive.

[63] *Op. cit.*

Additional References to the Medievalists

1531 Elyot, *Gouernour*, "Proheme" (end).
1551 Robinson, More's *Utopia*, Dedication (Bohn edition, p. 7).
1557 Tottel, *Miscellany*, Preface.
1561 Wilson, *Arte of Rhetorique*, Prologue (end of second paragraph).
1562 Heywood (John), *Proverbs and Epigrams* (Spenser Society, p. 174) Quoted by Watson, *Polybius*, "To the Reader."
1563 Googe, *Eglogs, Epytaphes, and Sonettes*, Dedication (Arber edition, p. 24).
1566 Partridge, *Historie of the most noble and valiant Knight Plasidas* (Collier, *Bibliographical and Critical Account*, 2:118).
1569 Jewel, *Works* (Parker Society, 3:140).
1569 Goosenius, *Zoilum Octastichon*, in Van der Noodt's *Theatre*.
[1570] Elviden, *The most excellent and pleasant Metaphoricall History of Pesestratus and Catena* (Collier, *ibid.*, 1:250).
1574 Rich, "Dialogue between Mercury and an English Soldier" (Collier, *ibid.*, 2:243).
1577 Northbrooke, *A Treatise against Dicing.* . . .
1578 Churchyard, *Description of the wofull warres in Flanders*, "To the Worlde."
1579 Spenser, *Shepheardes Calender*, "Immerito," "To His Booke," ll. 5-6.
1579 *Ibid.*, E. K., *Epistle* (Cambridge edition, p. 7, ll. 280 ff.).
1580 Lyly, *Euphues*, "To the Gentleman Scholars of Oxford" (Croll and Clemens edition, p. 184).
1581 Hall, *Iliad*, Dedication (see Wright, *op. cit.*, p. 134).
1581 Howell, *Devises*, "To the Reader."
1583 Stubbes, *Anatomy of the Abuses in England* (Furnivall edition, pp. ix, xiv, xix).
1586 Nashe, *Works* (McKerrow edition, 1:343; 2:183; 3:84, 315).
1588 Lloid, *Eiusdem in Zoilum*, in Kiffin's *Andria*.
1588 Greene, *Pandosta*, "Epistle."
1589 Spenser, *Faerie Queene*, "Dedicatory Sonnets": "Oxford," ll. 3-4; "Buckhurst," ll. 13-14.
1589 Bland, *A Baite for Momus* (*ad init.; ad finem?*).
1590 Lodge, *Rosalynde*, "To the Gentlemen Readers."
1591 Harington, *Orlando Furioso*, Preface (Gregory Smith, *ibid.*, 2:194-195).
1595 Lodge, *A fig for Momus*: "To the Gentlemen Readers Whatsoeuer"; "To Michael Drayton."
1595 Creede, W[arner's] Plautus, *Menaechmi*, "The Printer to the Reader."
1632 Parker (quoted in *Modern Philology*, 16:451).
(Probably a large part of Tupper's list cited above, p. 87, *supra*, note 15, might be included.)

Thus Googe exclaims,

> What shame shall this my ryme
> Receaue, that thus I publishe here in such a perlous tyme?[64]

[64] *Zodiake of Lyfe*, 1561 (Arber edition of *Eglogs*, p. 8). *Cf.* lines by Peend, p. 92, *supra*.

CHAPTER VI

POINTS AT ISSUE IN THE CONFLICT

The Alleged Grounds of Opposition

ON the other hand, the translators and the Zoili waged an open contest of exceedingly wide scope, practically all the issues of which, together with the arguments employed by either side in support of them, are available.

Legitimacy of Translation Challenged

FIRST, the medievalists uncompromisingly contended that nothing should be translated; and, to carry their point, they appealed to the superstitious fear of presumption and the awe for learning that had been inculcated in the minds of the laity during the middle ages. Dolman reports the opposition as saying that the translation of the classics was the

prophaning of the secretes of Philosophy, whiche are esteemed onelye of the learned, and neglected of the multitude. And therfore, vnmeete, to be made commen for euerye man.[1]

Aware from the early part of the century of the rationalistic nature of ancient literature, the men of the old order in Elizabeth's time clung to exclusiveness in learning as their last refuge, for

"Our men," says Hoby, "weene it sufficient to have a perfecte knowledge, to no other ende, but to profite themselves, and (as it

[1] *Tusculanae*, "To the Reader."

were) after muche paynes in breaking up a gap, bestow no lesse
to close it up againe, that others maye with like travaile folowe
after. . . . Our learned menne for the moste parte hold opinion,
to have the sciences in the mother tunge, hurteth memorie [*i.e.*,
tradition] and hindreth lerning."[2]

Giving the general public access to a rationalistic literature, beyond a doubt, put "Judicare in the Creede,"[3] and
presaged the certain disintegration of venerable institutions, mother church, the feudal system, and dialectic
philosophy.

By way of defense, Hoby categorically denied that
translating the classics did injury to tradition and learning, and pointed to the cultural progress that had been
made in other countries where the renaissance had flour-
ished.[4] Dolman[5] and Drant,[6] on the other hand, refused
to argue the matter, but regarded the classics as their own
best defense. Had the translators not won on this fundamental contention, the popular majority that supported
Elizabeth throughout her long reign might never have
been secured and the tendencies to revolt that periodically
made their appearance might not have been successfully
thwarted.

[2] *Courtier*, Dedication (*op. cit.*, p. 8).

[3] Gascoigne, "To al Young Gentlemen," Chalmers, *English Poets*, 2:
470.

[4] *I.e.*, Italy and France.

[5] "To those [the intelligent], I saye, there is nothing in this book to
darke. Especially, inasmuch as, the reading of one booke, will open an
other."—*Op. cit.*, Preface.

[6] "As for those who would haue nothing remoued from the natiue
tongue wherein it was written, because they dote more fullye, and grosly
then the reste, I woulde they had the greater parte of Heleborus. If
they vnderstande Latin I sende theim ouer to Tullies academicall ques-
tions, there to be assoiled of their so nyce a scruple. If they be meare
Englishe, and so in that case but *stantes pueri ad mensam*, their assertion is lesse autenticall, and I will dissemble my wante of an answer
whilste I heare further of ye pith of their profession."—*Horace*, "To the
Reader," 1567, *op. cit.*, p. 51.

Inaccuracy Charged

IN the second place, the Zoilists sought to discredit translations by declaring that the work done was inaccurate. Considerable dust is thrown into the air by the various translators' apologetic attitude. Neville, a very young man, coming very early in the period, apparently felt some reticence about the experiment of putting a Latin author into current English;[7] several others asked indulgence largely on personal grounds.[8] A few were aware of the general inadequacy of translation for conveying the meaning of the original texts, for Wilson confessed that both he and Cheke had been insufficient to the task.[9] But to the charge of the medievals that the translators made their books "invita . . . Minerva,"[10] or, in other words, were incompetent, certain ones retorted with feeling that if their critics were to undertake the work of translation,

[7] See p. 69, *supra*.

[8] Comparing his translation of Seneca with Heywood's and Neville's of the same author, Studley begs, "Take no offence that I (beinge one of the moste that can do least) haue thus rashly attempted so great an enterprise, to mingle my barbarusnes w^t others eloquencie."—*Agamemnon*, Preface (Spearing edition, p. 23). "I purposed accordinge to my sclender knowledge (though it were rudely, and farre disagreeyng from the fine and excellent dooinges now a dayes) to translate the same into our vulgar tongue."—Adlington, *Apuleius*, "To the Reader" (Seccombe edition, p. xxxv).

[9] "For this must I needes confesse, that I am altogither vnable to doe so in Englishe, as the excellencie of this Orator [Demosthenes] deserueth in Greeke. . . . And I thinke (although there be many doers) yet scant one is to be found worthie amongst vs, for translating into our Countrie speach. Such a hard thing it is to bring matter out of any one language into another," fol. 5b. "Maister Cheeke (whome I dare match with anye one before named for his knowledge in the Greeke tongue) hauing traueyled in Demosthenes as much as any one of them all, and famous for his learning throughout Europe: yet was he neuer so passing in his translations that no exception coulde be made against him."—*Demosthenes*, Dedication, fol. 5a-b. It will be noted that almost all the translators cited as apologizing for their work were university scholars. See also Harington, *Booke of Freendeship*, Dedication, 1550, Golding and Turberville, *passim*, who do not belong in that category.

[10] Turberville, "Rayling Route," l. 38.

they would find that they could do no better than the translators had done.[11] This does not seem like a very savage reply, but in it there was implied a reproof for cowardliness and neglect of duty toward country on the part of recognized scholars who did not translate but instead passed disdainful, embarrassing criticisms upon the work of those who did.[12]

In reality the contest at this point pertained to preserving the spirit of the original. The men of the inns of court refused to follow the pedantic requirements of the academicians, illustrated by the practices earlier employed in translating from one ancient language into another. These are described by Lockwood, as follows,

The translators seem almost to have regarded their task as the piecing together of a mosaic—word for word and phrase for phrase. And when an occasional technical term was left in its original Greek—or Arabic—form, no wonder that Roger Bacon could denounce the scholastic texts as barbarous and as falling far short of that lucidity which, if he could not know, he could at least divine. Thus the medieval translations owed their character to a peculiar purpose. They were not regarded as *belles lettres*. They were a means to an end—a purely professional end. Their language was the jargon of the schools: theological, philosophical, medical, mathematical.[12a]

In these new English translations, the scholastics not only

[11] "And if any with this will not be cōtented, than let hym take it in hand, & do it anew him self, and I nothing mistrust, but he shall finde it an easier thing to controlle a pece or two, than amende the whole of this enterpretacion."—Phaer, *Aeneid*, Preface.

> "For though the thing but slender be in sight,
> And vaine to vewe of curious carping skull,
> In mother tongue a foraine speach to write:
> Yet he shall finde he hath a Crow to pull,
> That vndertakes with well agreeing file
> Of English verse, to rub the Romaine stile."
> —Turberville, *Captious Sort*.

[12] See Dolman, pp. 89-90, *supra*. Cf. also Heywood, pp. 90-91, *supra*.
[12a] *American Philological Association*, 49:125.

failed to discover the "jargon," but they objected to the absolute transparency of the renditions. Their objection was not prompted, as it might seem, entirely by a pedantic interest, but by a further desire to assert the principle of special privilege. The ultimate intention was to render void the attempts of the new régime to create an enlightened public, by causing translated books to be unintelligible to common persons. An attempt made by Bishop Gardiner (1542) to destroy the larger influence of the *New Testament* by intercalating Latin words "that the people should not understand it much better for its being in English,"[13] illustrates what was intended. The demand for eloquence had the same object, for Roll, after discussing the assertion that, in comparison with ancient languages, English was barbarous, concludes his preface by saying,

Thou seest (good Reader) what a grounde they haue to defende their opiniō, and howe they labour only to roote out all good knowledge & vertue, and plāte mere ignoraunce amongest the common people.[14]

But the renaissance had become a matter of national import, and the translators insisted that the reading public should not be cheated out of what was due them. Googe's muse says to him,

[13] Burnet, *History of the Reformation* (Pocock edition, 1:498). The "justice" which Mullinger considers is due Bishop Gardiner (DNB) seems lightly deserved, for the twenty words given by Burnet of the hundred which Gardiner proposed to introduce, evidence the intention to ensconce Roman practice behind the language of the schools. Two years earlier Gardiner had put the liberal forces at Cambridge to rout. The More-Tyndale controversy concerned seven words, but upon them hung to a large degree the fate of the reformation. (*English Hexapla*, pp. 46, 49.) Bishop Tonstall (1526) found 2000 texts falsely translated in Tyndale's *New Testament* and More, 1000.

[14] *Logicke.*

> Turne my Poetes stately style,
> To Vulgar speche in natiue tounge: that all may vnderstand.[15]

Heywood, only, who evidently never quite severed his connections with the old order, was an exception whose procedure affords an interesting illustration of what the medieval critics expected. Between the time of his adherence to the translation movement and his subsequent entrance into the Society of Jesus at Rome, though still protesting against the strictures of the scholastics, he heeded them enough to submit to a change in his method of translation, which is described by his editor as follows:

Such places, where he "swerued from the trew sence" are rare in *Thyestes* and *Hercules Furens*. Whereas he added in *Troas* several scenes and choruses, he appends only one final soliloquy to *Thyestes*, and for the rest he keeps so closely to the original— especially in *Hercules Furens*—that he not only reproduces the Latin text verse for verse, but even in several instances the very order of the words in the verse. . . . Not only did he anglicize the Latin words of Seneca where he did not find an English term that corresponded, but he adopted the sententious style and inversions and intricate constructions of Seneca. In consequence his last two translations suffer from obscurity and entanglement.[16]

Had medieval "eloquence" been superimposed upon the

[15] *Zodiake of Lyfe*, Preface, 1561 (Arber edition of the *Eglogs*, p. 7). "How be it, I have not so exactly passed thorough the Author, as to pointe every sentence accordinge as it is in Latine, or so absolutely translated every woord, as it lieth in the prose, (for so the French and Spanish translators have not done) considering the same in our vulgar tongue would have appeared very obscure and darke, and thereby consequently, lothsome to the Reader, but nothing erringe as I trust from the given and naturall meaninge of the author, have used more common and familiar woords (yet not as muche as I might doo) for the plainer settinge foorthe of the same."—Adlington, *Apuleius*, "To the Reader" (Seccombe edition, p. xxxviii).

Cf. Cooper, *Bibliotheca Eliotae*, Preface, 1552, "*non verbum pro verbo anxie reddere, vt syllabas numerare videremur: sed vim vocibus subiectam pro viribus exprimentes, vtriusq; linguae gratiam et elegantiam seruare, praecipue studebamus.*"

[16] de Vocht, *Jasper Heywood and his Translations*, p. xxix; see also Spearing, *The Elizabethan Tenne Tragedies of Seneca*, pp. 441, 445, 446.

inchoate style demanded, the translators' work would have been lost in a heap of vacuities, and the translation movement would have come to a premature end. Instead, by preserving the spirit of the original in preference to the letter, and employing vernacular English, the men of the new order once for all opened the "gap" which the scholars had "closed."[17]

In order to aid the reader—while even according to the strict standards of today the translators were fairly literal—they also "interpreted" the texts,[18] *i.e.*, they included in the body of their work many explanatory items which the scholiasts had put in marginal notes, such as explanations of names and connecting links that facilitated the reading.

> Hydden storyes oft he showes, / to make his poet playne:
> (So as in double offyce he / might seeme for to remayne)
> As sometyme barely to expound, / to cōment sometyme eke,
> So that to vnderstand this booke, / ye neede no further seeke.[19]

In method as well as purpose they opposed the pedantic, exclusive scholars, since to them an ancient author was a wellspring of new life, not to be denied to anyone.[20]

[17] See pp. 102-103, *supra*.

[18] Several translators refer to themselves as interpreters. See dedications by Phaer, Hoby, Heywood (*Hercules Furens*), Wilson (*Demosthenes*), and Golding (*Psalms*); also Phaer's preface. Phaer cautions his readers that his *Vergil* is a translation, not a "construction," *i.e.*, a schoolbook.

[19] Nuce, verses prefixed to Studley's *Agamemnon*, ll. 31-38 (Spearing edition, p. 4). *Cf.* Studley, *Medea*, Preface (Spearing edition, p. 125).

[20] The objections made to the translation of the classics and of the *Old Testament* were identical. "These books . . . could never be put out of the way, neither by the hatred of any Porphyrian philosopher or rhetorician, neither by . . . the *envy* of the Romanists, and of such hypocrites who from time to time did ever bark against them, some of them not in open sort of condemnation, but more cunningly under subtile pretences; for that, as they were so *hard to understand*, and especially for that they affirm it to be *a perilous matter to translate* the text of holy Scripture, and therefore it cannot be well translated. And we

Works of Imagination Attacked

FAILING of success in direct assault upon the translation movement, the medievalists laid siege to some of the fundamental elements in the classics. The Protestant moralists had undertaken by means of *belles lettres* to transform the national mind and manners through the stimulation of the reflective and moral faculties. But purely literary writings were said by the opposition to be "frivolous and trifling toyes,"[21] and even "leasings"[22]—at least when attempted in English.[23] In other words, the free exercise of the imagination, like the employment of the individual judgment, was considered positively pernicious. Such an objection is hard to comprehend in view

may behold the endeavour of some men's cavillations, who labour all they can to *slander* the translators, to *find fault in some words of the translation*, but *themselves will never set pen to the book*, to set out any translation at all; they can in their constitutions provincial, under pain of excommunication, inhibit all other men to translate them."—Matthew Parker, Preface to the *Old Testament* (Robinson, *Fathers of the Church*, pp. 153-154). The italics are not in the original. For the complaint that the classics when translated were hard to read, see pp. 111-112, *infra*.

[21] "This spitfull Beast will (if he may) perswede
  That these are Toyes."

                    —Turberville, "Rayling Route," ll. 63-64.

"And so consequently, I to be had in derision, to occupy my selfe in such frivolous and trifling toyes."—Adlington, *Apuleius*, "To the Reader," *op. cit.*, pp. xxxv-xxxvi.

"I maye seeme to some, to haue taken in hand a vaine and friuolous trauell."—Golding, *Trogus*, "To the Reader."

"Neither be the thinges in him lighte trifles, excepte the lewde callynge them so can make them so, but euer emong he hath good, sounde, deepe, massye and wel rellest stuffe."—Drant, *Horace*, "To the Reader," *op. cit.*, p. 52.

[22] Both Elyot (*Gouernour*, 1:13) and Sidney (*Defense*, Cook edition, p. 34) mention this objection and some of the words of the translators probably imply it.

[23] With reference to prayers in the vernacular Harding, Jewel's controversial opponent, while protesting that he wished "that all the people understood all our prayers," thought "it not convenient in a common profane tongue to utter high mysteries. Therefore we wish they would learn the mystical tongue, and gladly do we teach their children the same."—Jewel, *Works*, 4:811.

of the unrestrained vagaries of medieval romance. But the classics, which directed attention to the world and the facts of human nature, were realistic and individualistic; the medieval romances, which dealt with abstractions and universals, were purely idealistic. Institutions founded upon authority might thrive under the influence of the latter, but the former implicitly contained the essence of Protestantism.

Two of the translators met these objections to classical poetry by stating an esthetic theory which in a measure anticipated Sidney's *Defense*. Golding affirmed that the method of poetry is sensuous elaboration, and its purpose to convey hidden truth.

For as the Image protrayed out in simple whight and blacke
(Though well proportioned, trew and faire) if comly colours
    lacke,
Delyghteth not the eye so much, nor yet contentes the mynde
So much as that that shadowed is with colours in his kynde:
Even so a playne and naked tale or storie simply told
(Although the matter bee in deede of valewe more than gold)
Makes not the hearer so attent too print it in his hart,
As when the thing is well declarde, with pleasant termes and art.
All which the Poëts knew right well: and for the greater grace,
As Persian kings did never go abrode with open face,
But with some lawne or silken skarf, for reverence of theyr state:
Even so they folowing in their woorkes the selfsame trade and
    rate,
Did under covert names and termes theyr doctrines so emplye,
As that it is ryght darke and hard theyr meening too espye.
But beeing found it is more sweete and makes the mynd more
    glad,
Than if a man of tryed gold a treasure gayned had.
For as the body hath his joy in pleasant smelles and syghts:
Even so in knowledge and in artes the mynd as much delights.
Wherof aboundant hoordes and heapes in Poets packed beene
So hid that (saving untoo fewe) they are not too bee seene.[24]

24 Golding, *Metamorphoses*, "To the Reader," ll. 119-138. Elyot's defense is similar. *Op. cit.*, 1 : 13.

Not only does poetry contain "darke and secret misteries
. . . counselles wyse and sage,"[25] but it has the quality
of universality.

And every other living wight shall in this mirrour see
His whole estate, thoughtes, woordes and deedes expresly shewed
    too bee.[26]

Moreover, the superiority of theology over poetry, admitted by Sidney, was not conceded by the translators, for
Drant, when reproved by his fellow clergymen for mis-
spending his time with translating the classics, boldly
declared that human nature, instead of being opposed to
the divine, was a way of approach to it.

He that woulde come to the vpmoste top of an highe hill, not
beinge able directly to go foreward for the steapnes thereof, if
he step a foot or twayne, or more oute of the way, it is not tho oute
of the waye for that it is a more conueyghable waye to the top of
the hill: so to cum to be able vtterers of the gospell, whiche is the
top, and tip of our climing, we must learne out of men to speake
according to the man, (which is a bystep from the pathe of
diuinitye,) yet very, and moste necessarye for that we that lyue
with men, speake with men, and preache to men. Thus therfore
for me to step asyde by melling with humanitye, is not to treade
out of my way, or lose my way, but to fynde my waye more ap-
paraunte reddie before me.[27]

Such an exposition of the office of poetry was wasted
on the Zoili, their followers and supporters, who were,
as Dolman said, "the raskall multitude." These, even
in many cases clergymen, found *Horace*, for example, when translated into English, very hard reading.
Drant, while baiting them under the sobriquet of "our
heuye frinde," very accurately sized up the mental state

[25] Golding, *Metamorphoses*, "To the Reader," 1. 187.
[26] *Ibid.*, ll. 195-196.
[27] *Op. cit.*, p. 52.

of the moderately intelligent among them, when he represented them as bewildered by the strangeness of the conceptions of classical literature, because they had an entirely different mental background from that of the men of the renaissance.

"But what if our heuye frinde," says Drant, with sarcastic play upon words, "haue a heauie heade, and an harde heade to ? What if he can perceaue my wordes, and not conceaue the Authors meaning ? It is hardlye sayd of him to say that I am harde, his owne witte being harde or the Author being harde for that he is not by him vnderstanded."[28]

One part of the reading public were beyond the pale; they were so dull that they did not perceive when a thing was written in jest or earnest, nor did they get subtle implications.

There are also certaine others, (hauing no skill at all) will yet be verie busie reading all that may bee read, and thinke it sufficient if (Parrot like) they can reherse things without booke; when within booke they vnderstande neyther the meaning of the Authour nor the sense of the figuratiue speeches.[29]

Such as these, who mistook "chalke for cheese" and the flitting of Camell and Churchyard for a story of a camel's straying into a churchyard, were representative of the products of medieval culture. That poetry presently began to flourish in a nation largely composed of such benighted individuals as these, constitutes a triumph for which the translators deserve no inconsiderable share of credit.

Immorality of Poetry Alleged

IN the next place, since in the matter of religion each side naturally regarded the other as fundamentally irre-

[28] *Op. cit.*, p. 53.
[29] Gascoigne, "To Al Young Gentlemen" (Hazlitt edition, 1:9).

ligious, the medievalists must have felt a considerable pleasure at being able to point out the heathen nature of the classics. The embarrassment that this objection caused the reformers is suggested by the fact that Studley, when publishing his *Medea*

chaunged the fyrste Chorus, because in it I sawe nothyng but an heape of prophane storyes, and names of prophane Idoles.[30]

On the other hand, Golding made two different defenses. Like Sidney he attempted to exonerate the ancient poets by declaring that not the classical authors but the traditions upon which they depended were at fault, adding that these were a version of the Scripture stories corrupted in transmission.[31] In almost, though not quite, Miltonic fashion, he also considered most of the heathen divinities symbolical of various human sins,[32] accompanying his theory with the exhortation,

But as there is no Christen man that can surmyse in mynd
That theis or other such are Goddes which are no Goddes by
    kynd:
So would too God there were not now of christen men profest,
That worshipt in theyr deedes theis Godds whose names they doo
    detest.[33]

By thus transforming the whole of mythology into an enlarged presentation of human activity, while he wholly ignored the measure of truth in his opponents' objection, he made way for the rationalistic view of morals.

Finally, on the question of the impurity of the classics,[34] though escape from the ultimate truth on this score

[30] Preface (Spearing edition, p. 126). *Cf.* Golding, *Metamorphoses*, "To the Reader," ll. 1-2.
[31] *Metamorphoses*, Dedication, 1567, ll. 338 ff.
[32] *Ibid.*, "To the Reader," ll. 58 ff.
[33] *Ibid.*, ll. 47-50.
[34] This objection of the medievalists to the classics is taken cognizance of in the *Gouernour*, l. 13.

was sought by some through a suppression of parts of the original texts[35] and by others through an appeal to allegory[36] (for which there was precedent in the medieval interpretations of Vergil, the fourteenth century *Ovid Moralizé*, and the Aldine edition of Ovid, authority and liberty, abstract idealism and rationalism, romanticism and realism), were again in direct opposition. Reason was made by Golding to dominate the passions. In the *Metamorphoses*,

The Authors purpose is too paint and set before our eyes
The lyvely Image of the thoughts that in our stomackes ryse.
Eche vice and vertue seemes too speake and argue too our face,
With such perswasions as they have theyr dooinges too embrace.
And if a wicked persone seeme his vices too exalt,
Esteeme not him that wrate the woorke in such defaultes too halt,
But rather with an upryght eye consyder well thy thought:
See if corrupted nature hane the like within thee wrought:
Marke what affection dooth perswade in every kynd of matter:
Judge if that even in heynous crymes thy fancy doo not flatter.
And were it not for dread of lawe or dread of God above,
Most men (I feare) would doo the things that fond affections move.[37]

The attitude toward evil assumed in the classics was held to be wholly different from that in the romances and bal-

[35] Drant, *Horace*, "To the Reader," 1566, *op. cit.*, p. 49.
[36] Golding, *Metamorphoses*, Dedication, ll. 63 ff. *Cf.* Adlington, *Apuleius*, Dedication (Seccombe edition, pp. xxxiii-xxxiv); Howell, *Fable of Narcissus*, Corser, *op. cit.*, 5 : 102.
[37] Golding, *Metamorphoses*, "To the Reader," ll. 151-162.
    "And sure these toyes, do showe for your behoof:
       The woes of loove, and not the wayes to love."
          —Whetstone, "A Remembraunce" (Chalmers, *English Poets*, 2 : 459). *Cf.* Turberville in Gascoigne's *Flowers*, 1572 (Hazlitt edition, 1 : xxxix).

    "So (gentle Reader) profite mayst thou gaine
    Of certaine Bokes which are some good, some yll
    Whereby with chaunge to recreate thy braine
    And it with sundrie sortes of matter fyll."
          —Sanford, *Plutarch*, "To the Reader."

lads. Examples of vices were considered essential to a complete moral education; and the ultimate responsibility for the use to which what was read was put, remained with the individual.[38] Between the translators and their opponents lay no middle ground; their views were irreconcilable. The one side proposed to burn the translations but were said by the other to

> overshoote themselves, and other folkes deceyve:
> Not able of the authors mynd and meening too conceyve.[39]

So positive at first were the liberals of the correctness of their attitude with reference to the moral character of the classics that they regarded those holding opposite opinions as wilfully perverse, giving them the epithet of "spiders" in contrast to intelligent readers, whom they denominated "bees." This terminology appears to have been common, and, owing to the difficulty of the situation, constituted almost the sole answer to this particular objection to the classics. In Fenton's *Certaine Tragicall Discourses* the reader is advised by one of the translator's friends,

[38] "Now too thintent that none have cause heereafter too complaine
Of mee as setter out of things that are but lyght and vaine:
If any stomacke be so weake as that it cannot brooke,
The lively setting forth of things described in this booke,
I give him counsell too absteine untill he bee more strong,
And for too use Ulysses feat ageinst the Meremayds song.
Or if he needes will heere and see and wilfully agree
(Through cause misconstrued) untoo vice allured for too bee:
Then let him also marke the peine that dooth therof ensue,
And hold himself content with that that too his fault is due."
—Golding, *ibid.*, ll. 213-222.

In the same year, 1567, Golding was publishing Calvin's book on *Offences* to teach the renunciation of impiety and worldly lusts (Epistle to Earl of Bedford). There can be then little doubt of his sincerity.

Sanford, who also feels the necessity of presenting both good and evil, takes as a motto "Tuto per il miglio." *Op. cit.*

[39] *Ibid.*, ll. 149-150.

Not for himself, thou knowest, it aunswered his delyght,
By skyll to understande the tale as dyd the aucthor write,
But, toylynge for thy syke, hath fourm'd his hyve ful fine.
Take thou the combe: the payne was his: the honye shal be thyne.
Good reader, yet beware, least spyder lyke thou take,
By cancred kynde a spightfull stynge, whence he did honye make.
Let not in lewe of payne, a tongue compleate with spyte
Attempt to harme (though powre shal want) the thing that he
    doth writ:

    .   .   .   .   .

For if thou dost, the wies will feele thy festred kinde;
And he to whom thou dost such wronge shal so thy nature finde.
No doubt our dayes are suche as every man can see,
And can at ease, and wyll, perceave the spider from the bee.
Let ZOILUS suck the teate, that Envie holdes in hell,
And say with me, "God spede the penn that hath begone so
    well."[40]

In refusing to recognize the heathen and immoral content of the classics, the translators were holding to the views of the earlier humanists and reformers; and had they not come to question their position in this matter, the history of English culture might have turned out quite differently.

Puritan Opposition

THE story of how the translation movement, which was begun by Puritans, was brought to an end by Puritans, is an interesting one. In the early seventies, although not all the classics had been rendered into English,[41] and some of the translators, like Golding, Drant, and Turber-

[40] Sir John Conway; see also Golding, *op. cit.*, ll. 163-168; Turberville, "Captious Sort," ll. 49-52; Gascoigne, "To the Reuerende Deuines," 1575 (Chalmers, *English Poets*, 2:468); Whetstone, "A Remembraunce," 1575, ll. 127-132 (Chalmers, *English Poets*, 2:460); *ibid.*, verses prefixed to Kendall's *Floweres*, 1577.

[41] The delay in the translation of such authors as Longus, Coluthus, Musaeus, Theocritus, Plautus, and Terence until several years later, indicated a principle of selection on the part of the early translators.

ville, had work still in progress, a considerable number of the men of the new movement turned their attention exclusively to making the continental reformers' writings available in English. Simultaneously the movement was deserted by its patrons. Cecil, who about the time of the Spanish crisis, or even before, had abandoned his republican leanings in governmental affairs and who still earlier had disappointed the hopes of the Calvinists by his trend toward Anglicanism, about 1566 appears to have ceased his active interest in the translation of the classics, particularly *belles lettres*.[42] Leicester was conniving with the Spaniards in order to further his project of marrying the Queen and hence was lacking in whole-hearted enthusiasm for liberal ideas. Norfolk, having become involved in the fortunes of Mary, Queen of Scots, lost his life at the block.

At the same time and perhaps in consequence of this changed attitude of the national leaders, there occurred a revival of medievalism throughout the nation. Church and state, assisted by the translators, had the popular majority necessary for conserving the work of the revolution. Yet the Queen and Cecil, too astute as politicians to be allured by the siren of pure idealism, knew how far to go; and in order to retain their constituency, now that it had been won, were willing to make concessions in the matters of ecclesiastical ritual and theology and felt the necessity of adopting a more autocratic attitude in civil govern-

---

[42] The date is that of Studley's *Agamemnon*, which was dedicated to Cecil, later considered an enemy of the poets. *Cf.* Spenser, *Faerie Queene*, opening of Book IV. In 1565, after addressing the Prime Minister in his *Caesar*, Golding, though perhaps still a resident at his patron's house, dedicated his *Metamorphoses* to Leicester, Cecil's political rival. Hall, though he had begun his translation in his youth while living under Cecil's roof, in 1581, dedicated it to the latter's oldest son, Sir Thomas. Wright, *op. cit.*, p. 132. *Cf. Shakespeare's England*, 2: 191-192.

ment. Hence, deprived of the support of civil and ecclesiastical institutions before the vast English public had been divested of their medieval modes of thought, the renaissance suffered a severe check. Further, with a large number of ancient classics available for general perusal, the inherent heathenism and immorality of ancient culture became too apparent to be longer overlooked.[43] For example, Underdown, when he republished his *Heliodorus*, hesitated to do so because of the immoral tone of his author,[44] and in 1575 Gascoigne, though still warring against the medievalists, accepted the Puritan strictures upon his *Flowers*. He says:

> But the third sort (being graue Philosophers, and finding iust fault at my doings at the common infection of loue) I must needes alledge such iust excuse as may counteruaille their iust complaints . . . finding by experience . . . how the first copie of these my posies hath been verie much inquired for by the yonger sort, and hearing likewise that (in the same) the greater part hath bin written in pursuit of amorous enterprises, they haue iustlie conceyued that the continuance thereof hath bin more likelie to stirre in all yong Readers a venemous desire of vanitie, then to serue as a common mirror of greene and youthfull imperfections.[45]

Accordingly, the translators, deprived of their earlier support and convinced of their error regarding the moral value of the classics, also abandoned the movement; and the Puritan party, being inundated with the uneducated, medievally-minded masses, now converted to Protestantism, assumed its better known obscurantist character.

---

[43] Ascham, too good a classicist to repudiate the ancients, in 1568 protested against the character of Italian writings, which to many of the translators were almost on a par with the works of antiquity.

[44] Dedication, 1587 (Whibley edition, p. 4).

[45] *Op. cit.* (Chalmers, *English Poets*, 2:471). "But I deeply regard the third." *Ibid.*, p. 470.

Finally, with the moral issue clearly drawn, the later con-
verts to the renaissance, who lacked the extreme conscien-
tiousness of the first translators, turned to the spread of
modern Italian literature, against which Ascham had been
the first to sound a warning.

This history of the relations of classicism and Puritanism is paralleled in the history of the drama. The early
Calvinist Protestants in England seem to have had no
compunction concerning plays and players. Bale, author
of several dramatic productions, among them *Kinge
Johan;* Udall, author of *Ralph Roister Doister;* Baldwin
and Ferrers, providers of entertainments at the court of
Edward, were Protestants of Puritan tendencies. In the
reigns of Henry and Mary, strolling players spread the
tenets of the reformation and suffered severely for doing
so.[46] In Elizabeth's time, Neville, Nuce, and Studley,
translators of Seneca; Sackville and Norton, authors of
Gorboduc; Broke, who translated and adapted *Romeus
and Juliet* to be acted at the Inner Temple; Golding,
whose knowledge of ancient drama was surprisingly accurate;[47] Gascoigne, translator of two plays and author
of another; and Elderton, Puritan, humanist sympa-
thizer, and actor,[48] exemplify the absence of prejudice
against plays and acting, such as was possessed by later
Puritans.[49]

[46] For acts and decrees against them on this charge, see Collier, *op.
cit.*, 2:384-385 (see under "Stalbridge"); Cal. State Papers, Dom., May
7, 1556.

[47] *Metamorphoses*, 3:126-128.

[48] See *Studies in Philology*, 17:199-245, and p. 75, *supra*. He ceased in
1562 to write the kind of ballads objected to by the translators.

[49] Gosson, who became prominent in the opposition to plays and
poetry, graduated from Oxford, the stronghold of reaction, in 1576.

Summary and Conclusion

AT the beginning of the present investigation it was proposed to take the statements of the translators at approximately their face value, and the reader cannot but have been impressed that the passages adduced in the course of the argument, even when bereft of their context, were the deliberate utterances of serious and purposeful men. From their testimony it is certain that the translators met with some sort of opposition—a fact which, once established, makes obligatory the discovery of the quarter from which the opposition arose and the grounds for the objections to translation. The task thus set has here been attempted, although the order of treatment has been reversed. Some of the evidence offered is cumulative rather than demonstrative in force, yet throughout theory and data have shown a surprisingly close relationship. To consider the translation of the classics important politically and socially is not easy without keeping clearly in mind the situation in the sixteenth century and the essential nature of the classics as well. Such has been the degree of human progress in the past four centuries that it is difficult to believe the right of the individual to exercise his reason and his imagination ever was considered a party issue; and such is present-day familiarity with classical culture that its essentially radical tendencies are no longer evident to all.

Early in the sixteenth century, medieval life in England was declining, although comparatively few signs of its immediate break-up were visible. Yet two forces that were soon to have a determining influence were present, humanism and a new aristocracy. Because of the belief in the exclusiveness of learning, the threat to the monarchy and the church was not clearly perceived. The reformation and the political events that followed, however, made both the new aristocracy and the new learning influences to be reckoned with. By the middle of the century, Protestantism, the renaissance forces, and the new nobility had come into alliance. At the universities the influence of the old learning persisted, but the liberal spirit had taken root. A portion, therefore, of the credit for the later triumph of liberalism and English liberty belongs to a now notable group of Cambridge scholars, who labored in the first half and middle of the sixteenth century.

At the time of the revolution under Edward the influential minority who then came into power and who were Calvinist Protestants, desirous of increasing political and intellectual freedom, recognized the value of the classics for propagating their principles. Owing to the decline in the use of spoken Latin and the correspondingly increased popularity of the vernacular—due to a growth of national feeling—they began, in emulation of other countries where the renaissance had taken root, to encourage the translation of ancient authors. After Mary's reign, which, though a time of trial both for Protestantism and the renaissance, caused only a temporary break in the progress of liberalism, the supporters of the new movement returned from contact with the continental reformers and humanists, or came out of retirement, to carry out the earlier program.

Beyond a doubt, unaided, the interest in the classics would have gradually grown, but at the beginning of

Elizabeth's reign members of the government and the Protestant leaders offered increased patronage to translators and, on account of the antagonistic attitude of the university scholars and the lack of renaissance scholars, sought out young, and for the most part untrained, men residing at the inns of court, and others, to make the classics available to the reading public. Hence there arose a "youth movement," not unlike youth movements in other periods of history, with characteristic exuberance, hostility to old ideas and institutions, and devotion to country and mother tongue.

The rationalistic element in the classics was looked to to overthrow feudal and medieval ideals and to nurture love of freedom and country; to strengthen Protestantism and improve morals; and to allay seditious tendencies. Culture and the general and literary use of unadulterated English were other desiderata. The ancients, moreover, were deemed the best teachers of military tactics. The wisdom of the program adopted was proved by subsequent events, for presently the nation reacted to the influence of classical literature, so that with the aid of other forces that operated simultaneously the initial ruling minority secured the support of a majority, Protestantism was established, and the general morale was raised sufficiently to withstand threat of invasion from without, to make rebellion fruitless, and to effect great national expansion.

Medievalism, however, did not succumb easily and indeed did not die. Continuing the policy and practices of the enemies of the new learning from the beginning, the reactionaries—scholastics, clergy, pamphleteers, and their followers—harried the men of the renaissance, and would have thoroughly intimidated the translators had the latter not been defended by the ruling nobles. The Zoilists, who were traditionalists with respect to all matters intellectual, cultural, ecclesiastical, moral, and political, and as such favored Papal and Spanish aspirations, condemned the work of translation altogether, attempted to destroy the value of translated works by means of pedantry, attacked *belles lettres*, and appealed to prejudice and passion. But they made a real impression only when they found the weak spot in the translators' armor; namely, the heathenism and the immorality of classical literature and culture. In the midst of the liberals' effort at destroying all things medieval, including medieval literature, when Protestantism and the new monarchy had reached a secure footing, the national leaders apparently felt that the new order had been carried far enough. Hence active suppression at an end, medievalism —greatly diluted, to be sure, with what the renaissance and the reformation had introduced into the national life —was once more permitted to become a dominating, though not wholly a dominant, force, so that ever since the pendulum has swung, sometimes in longer, sometimes in shorter arcs, between the extremes of romanticism and classicism in matters of thought and life.

The translation movement was more than an episode in English history; it was characteristic of a period, which, though brief, was germinal, as after-events have shown. For the moment, the entire reform party had identical interests and seemed in complete agreement. But presently, through the willingness of some in the complex Elizabethan public and the refusal of others to compromise, this unity was lost. In the church, the Anglicans readopted Roman practices, and the Puritan separatists staunchly declined to do so, with the result that an ecclesiastical *impasse* occurred that later caused serious religious and political disturbances. The government began again to employ autocratic methods in the face of strongly republican elements within the nation. Medieval moral criteria continued to be current even among the extreme Protestants, and medieval literature experienced a lusty revival in spite of the work that the translators had done. The first translators now abandoned translation to less inspired men at the inns of court,[1] and the propagation of the renaissance at the end of the century fell, for the most part, into the hands of men with less moral and religious purpose. Modern Italian culture, together with Italian modes of dress, Italian literature, and Italian low standards of morals came into vogue. Still out of all this intermixture and ferment, many great results in the fields of literature, commerce, war, and national progress came to pass.

Institutions of learning had been but slightly affected by the translation movement, and because of their reactionary trend in the sixteenth century, the universities of England for many generations were deprived of their due share in the national life. Even schools founded by Puritans in England and America have retained such a devotion to the classics in the original that frequently Cicero, Ovid, Vergil, and Horace have been little more than grammatical stalking-horses rather than the invigorating, refreshing stimulants to intellectual life that the first translators hoped that they would be.

Finally, owing to the peculiar position occupied by Puritanism in the translation movement and the renais-

---

[1] Nashe, *Works* (McKerrow edition, 3:315). Of course, Nashe could hardly have had in mind such an outstandingly excellent translator as North. Saville was not a member at the inns of court.

sance generally, it is possible to explain a curious phenomenon of history that is baffling to the uninitiated; namely, that the two more or less incoherent elements in Puritanism present at its beginning, Protestantism and humanism, have tended all along to produce two widely differing types of Puritans. One is the well-known obscurantist, inartistic, somewhat fanatical type, which has conserved much that was transferred to it from the middle ages. This class views life romantically and mystically, rather than rationally. Whether the Puritan devotion to a formal moral code is the outcome of medieval instruction or is characteristic of northern races, just as northern humanism differed in this respect from southern, is beyond the scope of this discussion. The other type, rarer but nevertheless common,—sometimes the same individual has belonged now to one and now to the other type,—is broadly liberal and rationalistic. Such as these, among whom were Spenser, Sidney, and Milton, have absorbed the spirit of the classics without violating their own moral sensibilities. In company with their forbears, the first translators, these have been among the proponents of the noblest freedom and the broadest culture.

APPENDIX

TRANSLATORS IN THE REIGNS OF EDWARD, MARY, AND ELIZABETH TILL 1572, ARRANGED ACCORDING TO DATES OF THEIR FIRST CLASSICAL TRANSLATIONS.

List complete from Nicolls (1550) through Churchyard (1572).

THE following data have been compiled chiefly from the *Dictionary of National Biography,* *Matriculations and Degrees, Cambridge* (Venn), *Register of the University of Oxford* (Boase edition, Vol. I), the registers of the inns of court—the Records of Gray's Inn (Foster), Middle Temple (Hopwood), Inner Temple (Inderwick), Lincoln's Inn (1896)—and Scott's *Elizabethan Translations* from the Italian. Other sources are usually cited. In determining an individual's religion, when it is not definitely known, his writings and activities have been taken into account. An asterisk (*) indicates conjecture, based in almost every case upon the sympathies of the author's patron or of his associates. For complete and accurate titles of classical translations, see Palmer, *op. cit.*; for those of other books, see DNB and Scott.

G.I. = Gray's Inn
I.T. = Inner Temple
M.T. = Middle Temple
L.I. = Lincoln's Inn
C = Roman Catholic
p = Protestant, interest moderate or unknown
P = zealous Protestant, usually Calvinist or Puritan

Translator	Classical Author	University Connection of the Translator	Membership at Inns of Court	Religion
Barclay	Sallust (1520?)			C
J. Rastell	Lucian (n.d.)		L.I.	C
W. Rastell (printer)	Caesar (1530)		L.I. 1532	C
Morison	Frontinus (1539)	Oxf. B.A. 1527/8	I.T. 1506	P
Cope	Livy (1544)	Oxf.		P
Burrant	Cato (1545)			P
Earl of Surrey	Vergil (c. 1548, 1557)			C
Nicolls	Thucydides (1550)	Camb. adm. 1544	M.T. pledge 1552	P*
Salisbury	Proclus (1550)	Oxf. 1540-7	Thavies' Inn c. 1547	P
			L.I. (?)	
Smyth	Herodian (1550?)	(a) Camb. B.A. 1541/2, M.A. 1545; Oxf. sup. B.A. 1546 (b) Oxf. B.A. 1545; sup. as M.A. for B.D. 1556		p*
Hill	Aristotle (1550?)		G.I. adm. 1531	
	Artemidorus, Ponzettus (1563)			
Lloyd	Hippocrates (1550?)	Oxf. B.A. 1547/8		p*
	Diocles (1550?)			
Harington	Cicero (1550)		M.T. 1509, 1510	p (P* ?)
Brend	Curtius (1553)			P*
	Caesar (unpub.)			

Translator	Classical Author	University Connection of the Translator	Membership at Inns of Court	Religion
Grimald	Cicero (1553); ? Philo (1563); ? Vergil (unpub.)	Camb. B.A. 1539/40 (DNB); Oxf. B.A. 1541/2; M.A. 1544		P-C
Paynell	Felicius (1541)	Oxf. (DNB)	G.I. adm. 1530	C-p
Wilson	Dares Phrygius (1553); Aristotle, Cicero, and Quintilian (1553); Demosthenes (1570)	Camb. B.A. 1546/7; M.A. 1549 (DNB); LL.D. 1571		P
Sherry	Cicero (1555)	Oxf. B.A. 1527 (DNB); M.A. 1531 (DNB)		
Bury	Isocrates (1557)	Camb. B.A. 1553 (DNB); M.A. 1555 (DNB)		
Phaer	Vergil (1558 and 1562)	Oxf. M.B. 1559; M.D. 1559	L.I.	(See p. 29, supra; p. 140, infra)
Blundeville	Plutarch (1558 and 1561); Aristotle (1599)	Camb. ? (DNB)	inn unknown (see p. 24, supra)	p*(P*?)
Anonymous	Artemidorus (1558/9)			
Heywood	Seneca (1559, 1560, 1561)	Oxf. B.A. 1553; M.A. 1558/9	G.I. adm. 1561 (see p. 141, infra)	C
Chaloner	Ovid (unpub.)	Oxf. ?, Camb. ? (DNB)	L.I. sp. pr. 1537/8	P
Googe	Aratus; Lucan (unpub. 1560 ?); Palingenius (1560, 1561, 1565)	Oxf, Camb. adm. 1555	Staples Inn c. 1560	P
Barker	Xenophon (1560)	Camb. M.A. 1540 (DNB)	M.T. expec. 1554/5; G.I. adm. 1561	p
Howell	Ovid (1560)			p*
Anonymous	Pythagoras (1560 ?)			
Anonymous	Isocrates (1560)			
Norton	Trogus Pompeius (1560)	Camb. adm. 1544; M.A. 1570	I.T. adm. 1555	P

Translator	Classical Author	University Connection of the Translator	Membership at Inns of Court	Religion
Dolman	Cicero (1561)	Oxf. B.A. 1557	I.T. adm. c. 1560	P*
Gilby	Cicero (1561)			P
Courtney	Plautus (1562)			C
Neville	Seneca (1563) Livy (unpub.)	Camb. B.A. 1559 (Spearing); M.A. 1581 (DNB)	G.I. by 1562	P
Whitehorne	Onosander (1563)		G.I. adm. 1543 (DNB)	
Haward	Eutropius (1564)	(Heward) Oxf. sup. B.A. 1559	Thavies' Inn	
Golding	Trogus Pompeius (1564) Caesar (1565) Ovid (1565, 1567) Seneca (1577) M. Pomponius and J. Solinus (1584)	Camb. mat. 1552	I.T. sp. pr. 1573/4 (G.I. visitor 1561; see p. 144, *infra*)	P
Evans	Horace (lic. 1564/5)	Oxf. (a) B.A. 1553/4; M.A. 1556; B.T. 1561/2 (b) B.A. 1565/6; M.A. 1570	See p. 145, *infra*	
Alday	Pliny (1565?)			
White	V. Flaccus (1565/6)		L.I. adm. 1552	P?
Peend	Ovid (1565)	(Pende) Camb. adm. 1559	M.T. adm. 1564	P*
A. O.	Lucian (1565)			
Drant	Homer (unpub.) Horace (1566, 1567) Cicero (lic. 1571)	Camb. B.A. 1560/1; M.A. 1564; S.T.B. 1569		P

Translator	Classical Author	University Connection of the Translator	Membership at Inns of Court	Religion
Adlington	Apuleius (1566)	Oxf. fellow		p (P*)
Nuce	Seneca (1566)	Camb. B.A. 1561/2; M.A. 1565; S.T.B. 1571/2		P
Studley	Seneca (1566, 1571)	Camb. B.A. 1566/7; M.A. 1570	Barnard's Inn c. 1566	P
Anonymous (probably Studley)	Seneca (lic. 1566/7)			
Painter	Latin historians (1566, 1567)	Camb. mat. 1554		p
Anonymous	Horace (1566/7)			
Anonymous	Cato (1566/7)			
Anonymous	Artemidorus (1566/7)			
San(d)ford	Plutarch, Heliodorus (1567) Epictetus (1567)	Oxf. ? (see p. 147, infra)		p
Turberville	Ovid (1567), (1565 ?) Vergil (1567) Lucan (by 1571, abandoned)	Oxf. (DNB)	inn unk. 1561 ?	p* or P* See p. 29, supra
Anonymous	Hippocrates (1567/8)			
Turner	Aetius, Galien (1568)	Camb. B.A. 1529/30 (DNB); M.A. 1533 (DNB)		P
Fulwood	Cicero (1568)		inn unk.	P*
Watson	Polybius (1568)	Camb. B.A. 1565/6; M.A. 1569	see p. 148, infra	P
Underdown	Heliodorus (1568/9) Ovid (1569)	Oxf. (DNB)	see p. 148, infra	P?

Translator	Classical Author	University Connection of the Translator	Membership at Inns of Court	Religion
Hubbard	Ovid (1569)		M.T. adm. 1571 (from Clifford's Inn)	
Stocker	Plutarch, Diodorus Siculus (1569)	Camb. mat. 1563		P
Newton	Cicero (1569); Rutilius Rufus (1580); Seneca (1581)	Oxf.; Camb. mat. 1562	G.I. adm. 1576 (fr. Barnard's Inn)	p
Blenerhasset	Ovid (unpub.)	Camb. (DNB)		
Billingsley	Epictetus (1570)	Camb. mat. 1551; Oxf. several years (DNB)		p
Candish	Epictetus (1570/1)	Camb. mat. 1569, no B.A.; M.A. 1572		P
Grant	Plutarch (1571)	Camb. B.A. 1567; M.A. 1573; Oxf. M.A. 1571/2		P*
Sadler	Vegetius (1572)	Camb. B.A. 1542/3; M.A. 1547	M.T. adm. 1566	P*
Anonymous	Martial (1571), (single sheet)			
Twyne	Dionysus (1572)	Oxf. B.A. 1564; M.A. 1568		
Gascoigne	Euripides (1572)	Camb. (DNB)	G.I. adm. 1555	P
Kenwelmersh	Euripides (1572)		G.I. adm. 1557	p
Churchyard	Ovid (1572)		I.T. adm. 1577	p
Baker	Galen (1574)		L.I. adm. 1540/1	
Roll	Aristotle (1574)		G.I. adm. 1565	P
North	Plutarch (1579)	Camb. (DNB)	L.I. adm. 1555/6	p
Hall	Homer (1581)	Camb. ? (DNB)	G.I. adm. 1556	p

Some of the friends of the new movement at the Inns.

Writer	Source of Material	University Connection	Membership at Inns of Court	Religion
Ascham	author	Camb. B.A. 1533/4 (DNB); M.A. 1537 (DNB)	M.T. 1554	P
Baldwin	author	Oxf. B.A. 1532/3	M.T. adm. 1557	P
Ferrers	author	Camb. B.C.L. 1537; Oxf. ? (DNB)	L.I. adm. 1534	P
Sackville	author	Oxf. ?; Camb. ? (DNB)	I.T. adm. 1555	P
Bavand	Ferrarius Montanus (1559)	Oxf. (DNB)	M.T. adm. 1557	p
Broke	Bandello (1562)		I.T. sp. pr. 1561/2	P
Hoby	Castiglione (1561)	Camb. adm. 1545; Oxf. (DNB)		P
Parker		Camb. B.A. 1562/3	L.I. adm. 1566	P*
Fenton	Bandello (1567)			P
Hake	à Kempis (1567)		G.I. c. 1567 (fr. Barnard's Inn)	
Yelverton	author	Camb. adm. 1550	G.I. adm. 1552	
Beverley	Ariosto (1566)	Camb. B.A. 1556/7	Staples Inn, by 1566	
Cavyll	author		M.T. 1552, 1570	

Other biographical and bibliographical data (selected)

Alexander Barclay (1475-1552)

c. 1514	author	*Eclogues*
1509	Brant (Locher)	*Ship of Fools*
1520?	Sallust	*Warre agaynst Iugurth*

John Rastell (d. 1536), a printer and lawyer, married Elizabeth, daughter of Sir Thomas More.

| n.d. | Lucian | *Necromantia* (selection) |

William Rastell (1508?-1565), son of the above, under Mary acted upon a commission of heresy and was appointed to a puisne judgeship, which he resigned in 1563 in order to retire to Louvain (see Jasper Heywood, *infra*).

| 1530 | Caesar | *Commentaries* (selection) |

Sir Richard Morison (d. 1556), early reformer and Calvinist, was active in governmental affairs under Edward, retiring to the continent during Mary's reign. A Greek scholar and the patron of Peter Martyr, he was intimate with humanists at home and abroad. He was one of Cecil's Lincolnshire friends (Hume, *op. cit.*, p. 31).

| 1539 | Frontinus | *Strategemes*, etc. |

Sir Anthony Cope (d. 1551), a courtier in the time of Henry, was a royal visitor to Canterbury and other dioceses under Edward. His son, by the same name, was imprisoned in the Tower (1587) for Puritan activities. (For declaration of the elder Cope's Protestantism see Livy, Dedication.)

| 1544 | Livy | *Books* xxi-ii | Henry VIII[1] |

[1] The names in the right-hand column are those of persons to whom the works were dedicated.

Robert Burrant (fl. 1553). (See p. 74 n., *supra*.)

1545   Cato   *Preceptes*   Sir Thomas Caverden, knt.

Henry Howard (1517?-1547), the famous Earl of Surrey.

c. 1548   Vergil   *Aeneid*, Book IV
1557   Vergil   *Aeneid*, Books II and IV

Thomas Nicolls (fl. 1550-1566, d. *ante* 1573) signed himself in 1550 "cytezen and goldesmyth of London." In 1566 he was Reader at his inn. (See *Thucydides*, t. p.; M.T. Records, 1 : 194.)

1550   Thucydides fr. French of Claude   *Hystory*   Sir John Cheke
          de Seyssel

William Salisbury (1520?-1600?), "the best philologist scholar among Welshmen of his time," lexicographer of eminence, and translator of the *New Testament* and part of the *Old Testament* into Welsh, while at Oxford was converted to Protestantism through the influence of Jewel. During Mary's reign he retired to Wales. His translation of Proclus appeared in the same year as his first anti-papal tracts.

1550   Proclus   *Description of the Sphere*   John Edwards of Chyrcke, Esquire

Nicholas Smyth

1550?   Herodian fr. Politian   *History*   Earl of Pembroke

Thomas Hill (fl. 1550?-1590) over a long period wrote for booksellers, and was the author of books on gardening and astrology. He practiced astrology.

1550?   Aristotle and others (fr. B. Cocles)   *Phisiognomie*   George Keable, Esquire
1563   Ponzettus and Artemidorus   *Interpretacion of Dreames*   George Keable, Esquire
1576   (another edition)

Humphrey Lloyd (d. 1570) was "in much esteem for his great knowledge of British antiquities." (Foster, *Alumni Oxonienses.*)

1550?	Hippocrates, Diocles, and others fr. Lat. of Hyspanus	*Treasury of Healthe*	Master William Cecil, Esquire

John Harington (fl. 1550), father of Sir John Harington, the poet (see Park, Vol. 2), is said to have married for his first wife a natural daughter of Henry VIII, and for his second a lady in waiting on the Princess Elizabeth at Hatfield (1554). He was in the employ of Henry,—John Bradford, the future martyr, being his clerk. At one time he suffered imprisonment in the Tower with Elizabeth. His patroness was mother of the youthful and much-lamented "Dukes of Suffolk," Henry and Charles Brandon, promising pupils of Thomas Wilson (*q.v.*). The DNB does not seem to notice Harington's translation of Cicero.

1550	Cicero	*Freendship*	Catherine, Duchess of Suffolk

John Brend (d. 1565?) appears in *Middle Temple Records* as *John Brent.* (See p. 47, *supra.*)

1553	Quintus Curtius	*Historie*	Duke of Northumberland
1564	Caesar	*Commentaries* (4½ books) unfinished.	

Nicolas Grimald (1519-1562), an active scholar and man of letters, became rhetorical lecturer at Oxford beginning in 1544. During Edward's reign he was prominent in his support of the revolution, but later became infamous to the Protestants by furnishing the evidence that sent Ridley and Latimer to the stake. (Merrill, PMLA, 37 O.S. 216-227.)

1553	Cicero	*Duties*	Thomas Thurley, Bishop of Ely
1555	reputed author	*Institution of a Gentleman*	Lord Fitz-Walter
1557	author	Poems in Tottel's Miscellany	Queen Elizabeth
1563	Philo fr. Lat. of Humphrey	in *Of Nobles and Nobility*	
(very doubtful)	Vergil	**?** (only referred to by Googe ; see p. 20, *supra*)	

Thomas Paynell (fl. 1528-1567), chaplain to Henry VIII and adherent of the house of Montague, was probably only a lukewarm Protestant (see his profession of Catholicism in *Conspiracie of Cataline*, Dedication, 1557), and perhaps not a whole-hearted humanist (*cf.* his advocacy of "eloquence," p. 13, *supra*). He held church livings under Elizabeth, and was a prolific translator of various types of writings.

1541	Felicius	*Conspiracie of Cataline*	Henry VIII
1557		another edition	Viscount Montague
1553	Dares Phrygius	*Destruction of Troy*	Sir John Browne
1561	Hanape	*Examples of Vertue out of Scripture*	Queen Elizabeth
1562		*Commonplaces in St. Paul's Epistles*	Thomas Argall
1567/8	(assigned by Stat. Reg.)	*Amadis of Fraunce*	

Thomas Wilson (1525?-1581), a Cambridge scholar and a close friend of Cecil, Cheke, and Smith, from 1560/1 acted as ambassador, member of Parliament, examiner of prisoners taken at the time of Norfolk's arrest, and Secretary of State (1577-81). From 1553 Wilson was also "a staunch adherent of the Dudley family."

1551	author	*Arte of Logic*	Edward VI
1553	Aristotle, Cicero, Quintilian (Mair, p. xxxv)	*Arte of Rhetorique*	Earl of Warwick, eldest son of Duke of Northumberland
1561		another edition	
1572 (Pref. 1569)	author	*Discourse on Usury*	Earl of Leicester
1570	Demosthenes	*Orations* (7)	Sir William Cecil

Richard Sherry (c. 1506-post 1555) from 1534 to 1540 was headmaster of Magdalen College, Oxford.

| 1555 | Cicero | *Oration of Marcus Marcellus* in *Figures of Grammer and Rhetorike* | Sir W[illiam] Chester |

John Bury (fl. 1557) was the nephew of his patron.

| 1557 | Isocrates | *Demonicus* | |

Thomas Phaer (1510?-1560), earlier a writer of legal and medical books, was friend of Ferrers (a member of Lincoln's Inn), who, with Baldwin (*q.v.*) was a provider of entertainment at the court of Edward, both of them vigorous Protestants and contributors to the *Mirror for Magistrates*. Phaer's Catholicism is alleged chiefly on the basis of an ambiguous provision of his will. (See Thomas Twyne, *infra.*)

| 1558 | Vergil | *Aeneid* (eight books) | Queen Mary |
| 1562 | Vergil | *Aeneid* (nine and a half books) (posthumous) | Sir Nicholas Bacon (dedication by printer) |

Thomas Blundeville (fl. 1561). Verses by T. B. appear in Studley's *Agamemnon* (Spearing edition, pp. 16-18) and Gascoigne's *Posies* (Chalmers, *English Poets*, 2: 475). (See p. 24, *supra.*) Ascham contributed verses to Blundeville's Plutarch (1561).

(lic.) 1558/9	Plutarch		Earl of Leicester
1561	Plutarch	*The Fruit of Foes* *Three Moral Treatises*	(1 and 2) Queen Elizabeth (3) John Astley and John Harington
1565, 1566	author	*Horsemanship*	Earl of Leicester
1570	Federigo Furio	*Counsels of a Prince*	Earl of Leicester
1570	John Sturmius	*A rich Storehouse*	
1599	Aristotle	*Logike*	

Jasper Heywood (1535-1597/8), son of the well-known John Heywood, grandnephew of Sir Thomas More, nephew of William Rastell (q.v.), page to Princess Elizabeth, and Oxford scholar, though "a steady catholic" (Pole) seems to have been on the best of terms with the members of the new government and the translators at the inns of court as early as 1560, perhaps before. But see p. 29, *supra*. He certainly was at the inns of court as early as 1560, perhaps before (*cf.* Graves, *Modern Philology*, 10: 568).

1559	Seneca	*Troas*	Queen Elizabeth
1560	Seneca	*Thyestes*	Sir John Mason
1561	Seneca	*Hercules Furens*	Earl of Pembroke

Sir Thomas Chaloner (1521-1565), almost continuously in government employ from the time of Henry, was active in the revolution, testifying against Bonner and Gardiner, and was a trusted agent of Elizabeth. He had a reputation as a man of letters.

1559	author	*Mirror for Magistrates* ("Mowbray")	
1878	Ovid	*Epistolae Heroidum* (Epistle 17)	

Barnabe Googe (1540-1594), kinsman of Cecil, cousin of Neville (q.v.), and friend of Turberville (q.v.), held a prominent place in the new literary movement. (See p. 24, *supra*.)

(unp.)	Aratus	(abandoned)	
(unp.)			
1560	Lucan	*Pharsalia* (abandoned)	
1560	Palingenius	*Zodiake of Lyfe* (3 books)	Lady Hales (grandmother) and three others (lawyers)
	(Manzoli, fl. 1534-59)		
1561	Palingenius	*Zodiake of Lyfe* (6 books)	Sir William Cecil
1563	author	*Eglogs, Epytaphes, and Sonettes*	William Lovelace Reader, Gray's Inn
1565	Palingenius	*Zodiake of Lyfe* (complete)	Sir William Cecil
1570 } one	Kirkmayer	*The Popish Kingdome or Reigne of Antichrist*	Sir William Cecil
1570 } vol.	Naogeorgus	*Spiritual Husbandrie*	Queen Elizabeth

William Barker (fl. 1572), educated in Cambridge at the cost of Anne Boleyn, later attended the university at Florence. He served as member of Parliament, 1557-1559, 1571, and also acted as secretary to the Duke of Norfolk. His literary activities were considerable. In 1571 his evidence sent the Duke of Norfolk to the block (*Nobility of Women*, Bond edition, p. 1).

1904-5	(ms. 1559) Agrippa Capella	*Nobility of Women*	Queen Elizabeth
1560	Xenophon	*Cyropaedia*	Earl of Pembroke
1567	another edition	*Cyropaedia*	Philip, Earl of Surrey (s. of Duke of Norfolk)

Thomas Howell (fl. 1568) spent most of his life as secretary in the households, successively, of the Earl of Shrewsbury and the Countess of Pembroke. His patroness was the daughter of the Earl of Pembroke and the daughter-in-law of the Earl of Shrewsbury.

1560	Ovid	*Metamorphoses (Narcissus)*	Maister Henry Lassels, Gentelman
1567/8	author	*Newe Sonets and Prettie Pamphlets*	
1568	author	*The Arbor of Amitie*	Lady Ann Talbot

Thomas Norton (1532-1584), one-time amanuensis to the Duke of Somerset, son-in-law of Archbishop Cranmer, entered Parliament in 1571. He was praised by Bacon and Cecil for his fidelity to prince and country.

1557	author	Tottel's *Miscellany* (one poem)	
1560 ?	Trogus Pompeius	*Oration of Arsanes against Philip*	
1565	author	*Gorboduc*, Acts 1-3	
(played 1561)			
1561	Calvin	*Institutes*	

John Dolman (fl. 1561)

1559	author	*Mirror for Magistrates* ("Hastings")	
1561	Cicero	*Tusculanian Discourses*	Bishop Jewel

Goddred Gilby (fl. 1561), son of a famous Puritan divine, was with his father in Geneva during Mary's reign.

1561	Cicero	*Epistle to Quintus*

Edward Courtney (1526?-1556), Duke of Devonshire, though a Catholic in Mary's reign, headed the anti-Spanish party. By them he was proposed as the husband of Elizabeth. Sir Thomas Wyatt perished in an attempt to raise him to the throne.

1562/3	Plautus	*Amphitryo*

Alexander Neville (1544-1614), cousin of Googe (*q.v.*), to whose *Eglogs* (1563) he contributed, became secretary successively to Archbishops Parker, Grindal, and Whitgift. His brother, Thomas, actively defended Puritanism at Cambridge in 1595. (For his membership at Gray's Inn, see Chalmers, *English Poets*, 2: 449.) (Spearing, *Elizabethan Translations of Seneca's Tragedies*, p. 20.) The translator states that he translated *Oedipus* to be acted at Cambridge (Dedication).

1563	Seneca	*Oedipus*	Dr. Wotton
(translated in 1560)			
1576	Livy	unpublished	

Peter Whitehorne (fl. 1543-1563). See p. 47, *supra*.

1560-62	Machiavelli	*The Arte of Warre*	Queen Elizabeth
(t.p. 1560, col. 1562)			
1563	Onosander (fr. Fabio Cotta's Ital.)	*Onosandro Platonico of the General Captaine*	Duke of Norfolk

Nicolas Haward (fl. 1569)

1564	Eutropius	*Chronicle of the Romans*	Maister Henry Compton, Esquire

Arthur Golding (1536?-1605?), uncle of the seventeenth earl of Oxford (admitted to Gray's Inn 1561) and a companion of the latter during his minority, was for a time a resident at the house of Cecil (see *Metamorphoses*, 1565, Dedication), who was the Master of the Queen's Wards. The translator, therefore, must have very early had a circle of acquaintances at the inns. (See pp. 41, 47, *supra*.) John Golding, the poet's father, under Henry, was one of the auditors of the Exchequer and a Middle Templar (adm. 1520).

Year	Author	Work	Dedicatee
1563	Aretino (Leonardo) (D. Bruni)	*Warres of the Gothes*	Sir William Cecil
1564	Trogus Pompeius	*Histories*	Earl of Oxford
1565	Ovid	*Metamorphoses* (four books)	Earl of Leicester
1565	Caesar and Hirtius	*Commentaries*	Sir William Cecil
1567	Ovid	*Metamorphoses* (fifteen books)	Earl of Leicester
1567	Calvin	*Offences*	Earl of Bedford
1570	Chytraeus	*A Postel*	Sir Walter Mildmay
1571	Calvin	*Psalms*	Earl of Oxford
1572	Beza	*Christian Questions and Answers*	Earl of Huntingdon (see under Hoby, *infra*)
1577	Seneca	*Offices* ("Benefits")	Sir Christopher Hatton
1585	Mela Pomponius and Juslius Solinus (extract from Pliny)		

Lewis Evans is the name of two different persons noticed by Foster (*Alumni Oxonienses*). One of them was a Catholic in flight at the time the translation of Horace, which may never have been printed, was licensed. He later embraced Protestantism, and both men took orders. The author of the *Castle of Christianitie* is identified by DNB with the first of the two mentioned above. The translator is designated on the title page as "schole-maister." (See Palmer, pp. xv, 62.)

	Horace	Satires (two)	Queen Elizabeth
(lic.) 1564/5	author		
1568		*Castle of Christianitie*	

John Alday (fl. 1570).

	Pliny (Secundus)	*Antiquities*	
1565?			
(lic.) 1566	Boaistuau	*Theatre Mundi*	Sir William Chester

Sir Nicholas White (d. 1593), a descendant of one of the Pale settlers in Ireland, spent much of his life in that country in government employ, in association with the Earl of Ormonde, a staunch Protestant and in the sixties a favorite at the English court.

1565/6	Flaccus	*Jason and the Golden Fleece*	

Thomas Peend (fl. 1564-1566)

	Ovid	*Metamorphoses (Hermaphroditus and Salmacis)*	Nicholas St. Leger
1565			
1565	founded on Bandello (fr. Spanish) author	*John Lord Mandosse*	Sir Thomas Kemp, knight (kinsman)
1566		Verses in Studley's *Agamemnon*	

Thomas Drant (d. 1578?) was domestic chaplain to Archbishop Grindal and reader at St. Paul's. He was a classical scholar and a pronounced Puritan. He advocated classical rules for English versification.

unpub.	Homer	five books	
1566	Horace	Satires	Ladies Cecil and Bacon
1566/7	Horace	Art of Poetry, Epistles and Satires	Earl of Ormonde
1571	Cicero	Archias	

William Adlington

| 1566 | Apuleius | The Golden Ass | Thomas Radcliffe, Earl of Arundel (Sussex) |

Thomas Nuce (d. 1617), rector in Norfolk and Suffolk, made his translation of Seneca before leaving Cambridge. From 1584/5 till his death, he was Prebend of Ely cathedral.

| 1566 | Seneca | Octavia | Earl of Leicester |

John Studley (c. 1547-1590) was a Puritan, follower of Cartwright, and during the years 1569-1572 took part in the struggle at Cambridge against Whitgift. The verses by his friends in his translations show an early intimacy with members of the inns of court. (See also Spearing edition, pp. ix-xi, xxii-xxiii.) (Spearing, Elizabethan Translations of Seneca's Tragedies, p. 36.)

1566	Seneca	Agamemnon	Sir William Cecil
1566	Seneca	Medea	Earl of Bedford
1571	Seneca	Hercules Oetaeus	
prob. 1566/7	Seneca	Hyppolytus	

William Painter (1540?-1594) most of his life was clerk of the ordnance in the Tower of London under the Earl of Warwick and Sir George Howard. He seems to have begun translating classical authors as early as 1561. (Jacobs edition, p. xxvi.) The date, c. 1525, suggested by Jacobs (p. xxiv) for Painter's birth appears to be simply a guess.

| 1566 | Gr. Lat. and renaissance writers | Palace of Pleasure, Pt. 1 | Earl of Warwick |
| 1567 | | Palace of Pleasure, Pt. 2 | Sir George Howard |

James San(d)ford (fl. 1567) presented his *Epictetus* at Oxford at the time of the Queen's visit in 1567. (G. Plummer: *Elizabethan Oxford Reprints*, p. 183.) In 1586 he became tutor to the third Earl of Pembroke, the nephew of Leicester.

1567	Plutarch, Heliodorus	*Amorous and Tragicall Tales* *Cariclea and Theagenis*	Sir Hugh Paulet of Hinton St. George, Somerset
1567	Epictetus	*Manuell*	Queen Elizabeth
1569	C. H. Agrippa	*Of the Vanitie and Uncertaintie of the Artes and Sciences*	Duke of Norfolk
1573	(compiler)	*Garden of Pleasure*	Earl of Leicester

George Turberville (1540?-1610?) was on intimate terms with Googe, Gascoigne, and Fenton. In 1568 he accompanied Thomas Randolph to Russia as secretary of an ambassadorial mission. Rollins merely conjectures from the activities of his family that Turberville was a Catholic (*Mod. Phil.* 15 : 527), but see p. 29, *supra*.

1567 (1565?)	Ovid Aulus Sabinus } one volume	{ *Heroycall Epistles* *Answers*	Thomas Howard, Viscount Bindon
1567	Vergil	*Eclogues*	
1567	Mantuan author	*Eglogs*	
1567		*Epitaphes, Epigrames, Songes and Sonets*	Hugh Bamfield (uncle)
(1565?)			Countess of Warwick
1568	Mancinus	*Plaine Path to perfect Vertue*	Countess of Warwick
before 1571	Lucan (abandoned)		Earl of Warwick (intended)

William Turner (d. 1568), clergyman and distinguished scientist, a zealous follower of Ridley and Latimer, fell under persecution in Henry's reign. He was chaplain and physician to the Duke of Somerset and lived abroad during the time of Mary. Later, as a Puritan, he was suspended from his deanship of Wells for his non-conformity.

1568	Galen and Aetius	*Nature of Wines*	Sir William Cecil
1568	author	*A New Herbal*	Queen Elizabeth

William Fulwood (fl. 1562). (See Richard Robinson, *Rewards of Wickedness*, quoted by Spearing in *Studley's Translations*, p. xii.) His translation is not cited by Palmer.

1563	Bergomatis	*Castel of Memorie*	Earl of Leicester
1568	Cicero	*Enemie of Idlenesse*	Company of Merchant Taylors

Christopher Watson (d. 1581) was among the opponents of the new Cambridge statutes of 1572. At one time a rector, he spent much time at the home of his patron, who was a judge of the Queen's Bench and in 1561 Treasurer of the Inner Temple and through whom he may have been introduced at the inns of court.

1568	Polybius	*Histories*	Thomas Gawdy, Esquire

Thomas Underdown (fl. 1566-1587) is little known except for his translations. "No one knows whether he betook himself to the church or spent a more adventurous life in the courts."—Whibley, *Heliodorus* (Tudor Translations, Preface). His invective against vice, though directed against women, suggests Puritan tendencies (see Collier, *op. cit.*, 2:74-76).

1566	Ovid (Whibley)	*Theseus and Ariadne*	Earl of Oxford
1568-9	Heliodorus	*Ethiopian History*	Sir Thomas Sackville
1569	Ovid	*Ibis*	

William Hubbard

1569   Ovid   *Metamorphoses (Ceyx and Alciene)*

Thomas Stocker (fl. 1569-1592)

1569   Plutarch, Diodorus Siculus   *History of the Successors of Alexander* Earl of Warwick

Thomas Newton (1542?-1607), a rector, was also writer of historical, medical, and theological works and of Latin verse. He is best known as the compiler of the *Tenne Tragedies of Seneca* (1581), in which are contained the plays already translated by Heywood, Neville, Nuce, and Studley, and for which he translated the *Thebais*. (Palmer wrongly attributed the *Paradoxes* and *Scipio's Dream* to Thomas Norton.)

1569   Cicero   *Of Old Age*   Marquis of Winchester
1569   Cicero   *Paradoxes* and *Scipio's Dream*   Sir Walter Mildmay
1580   Rutilius Rufus   *Wars of Romans and Carthaginians*

Thomas Blenerhasset (1550?-1625?)

unpub. Ovid   *Remedio Amoris*
1578   author   *Mirror for Magistrates* (Continuation
                                of Second Part)

Henry Billingsley (d. 1606) was a wealthy merchant and in 1596 became Lord Mayor of London. Foster (*Alumni Oxonienses*) accords him the title of "sir."

1570   Epictetus   *Geometrie*

Richard Candish (d. 1601?); (fl. 1556, Palmer), has here been taken to be the same as Richard Cavendish (DNB), (Venn and Venn).

1570/1 Epictetus   *Geometry*

Edward Grant (1540?-1601), scholar, Latin poet, for twenty years headmaster of Westminster school, and in later life successively vicar, rector, and sub-dean at Westminster Abbey, was an admirer of Ascham and Jewel, as his verses lamenting their deaths show.

1571	Plutarch	*Training of Children*

John Sadler (d. 1595?) for many years previous to 1571 enjoyed a liberal bounty from Francis Lord Russell, second Earl of Bedford. To his translation of Vegetius are prefixed verses by Drant, and other Cambridge men. His associates suggest a sympathy with both humanism and Puritanism.

1572	Vegetius	*Martiall Policye*, etc.	Earl of Bedford

Thomas Twyne (1543-1613)

1572	Dionysus	*Survey of the World*	William Lovelace, Esquire
1573	Vergil, Maphaeus	*Aeneid* (Books 9b-13)	Lord Buckhurst (Sir Thomas
		(Completion of Phaer's translation)	Sackville)

George Gascoigne (1525?-1577) was soldier and member of parliament (1557). *Supposes* was written to be performed at Gray's Inn, Francis Kenwelmersh contributing Acts 1 and 4. Gascoigne in later life became a pronounced Puritan. (*Camb. Hist. of Eng. Lit.*, 3:233.) (See p. 98 n., *supra.*)

1566	Ariosto	*Supposes* (*Gli Suppositi*)
(Played 1566)		
1572	Euripides (fr. Dolce's Ital. of	*Jocasta*, Acts 2, 3, 5
	The Phoenissae)	
1572	Various classical and renaissance	*Posies*
	authors	

(Played 1566)

1572   Euripides (fr. Dolce's Ital.)   *Jocasta*, Acts 1 and 4

Thomas Churchyard (1520?-1604), was a soldier and a voluminous, though far from brilliant, writer. (See pp. 41-42, *supra*.)

1557	author	Poems in Tottel's *Miscellany*	
1563	author	*Mirror for Magistrates* ("Shore's Wife")	Sir Christopher Hatton
1572	Ovid	*De Tristibus*	
unpub.	Pliny	portion unknown	
unpub.	Vergil	portion unknown	

Henry Baker

1574   Galen   *Pricks and Wounds*

Maurice Roll

1574   Aristotle (Ramus)   *Logicke*

Sir Thomas North (1535-1601?). Upon her release from the Tower, Elizabeth was entertained at North's father's house, now Charterhouse, London.

1557	Guevara	*Diall of Princes* (See p. 18 n., *supra*)	Queen Mary
1570	"auncient writers" (fr. Ital.)	*Philosophy of Doni*	
1579	Plutarch (fr. French of Amyot)	*Lives*	Queen Elizabeth

Arthur Hall (1539-1605), one of Sir William Cecil's wealthy wards, in early years lived at Cecil's house in company with the Earl of Oxford and the latter's uncle, Arthur Golding (*q.v.*). At the inns of court he enjoyed the acquaintance of Sir Roger Ascham and Jasper Heywood. (Wright's *Life and Works of Arthur Hall*, pp. 20, 36.)

1581   Homer   *Iliad* (ten books)   Sir Thomas Cecil

Roger Ascham (1515-1568) before 1550 was a prominent Greek scholar at Cambridge and for a time tutor of Princess Elizabeth. In that year he accompanied Sir Richard Morison (q.v.) to the court of Charles V. Though a Protestant and Puritan he was Latin secretary to Queen Mary.

1545	author	*Toxophilus*	Henry VIII
1570	author	*Scholemaster*	Sir William Cecil
(1568)			

William Baldwin (fl. 1547), printer associated with Whitchurch and Wayland, provider of entertainments for the court of Edward, and Protestant satirist, led in the production of the *Mirror for Magistrates*. (See p. 24, *supra*.)

1559		*Mirror for Magistrates* (chief contributor)	"To all the nobilitie"
1563		*Beware the Cat*	John Young
1561?	author		
1570			

George Ferrers (1500?-1579). See Phaer, *supra*.

| 1559 | author | *Mirror for Magistrates* |
| 1563 | | |

Sir Thomas Sackville (1536-1608) (later Lord Buckhurst) was closely connected with the new régime through the political activities, from first to last, of his father, who was a member of the Queen's Privy Council (at one time Reader at Gray's Inn). Upon being knighted in 1567, Buckhurst was hailed as a real addition to the Protestant party in the House of Lords. He enjoyed a reputation for his Latin and English compositions, which have been lost. (See p. 24, *supra*.)

1559, 1563	author	*Mirror for Magistrates* ("Buckingham" and "Induction")
1561	author	*Gorboduc*, Acts 4, 5
1561	author	Prefatory verses to Hoby's *Courtier*

William Bavand. His author was a noted humanist (at one time lecturer on civil law) of the University of Marburg, who had been educated under Melanchthon at Wittenberg. (*Allgemeine Deutsche Biographie.*) (See p. 24, *supra.*)

1559   Ferrarius Montanus   *Ordering of a Common Weale*   Queen Elizabeth

Arthur Broke (d. 1563), admitted to the Inner Temple in recognition of his plays composed for performance at the Inn, was drowned en route to foreign military service and was subject of an elegiac poem by Turberville. (See pp. 26 n., 119, *supra.*)

1562   Bandello (fr. French of Boaistuau and Belleforest)   *Romeus and Juliet*

Sir Thomas Hoby (1530-1566), an active Protestant, friend of Ascham and Cheke, was a foreign ambassador under the Edward and Elizabeth. He was "expert in the knowledge of divers tongues" and forcefully defended the translation of the classics (see pp. 67-68, 102-103, *supra*). His wife was Elizabeth Cooke. (See p. 41 n., *supra.*) Lord Henry Hastings, Earl of Huntingdon, son-in-law of the Duke of Northumberland, because of descent from Edward IV, was looked upon as a possible successor to the throne. "He was conspicuous by his lavish support of those hot-head preachers." (Tudor Translations, p. xxxix.)

1561   Castiglione   *Courtier*   Lord Henry Hastings, Earl of Huntingdon

William Parker

1566   Verses in Studley's *Agamemnon and Medea*

Sir Geoffrey Fenton (1539?-1609), related to Cecil and Leicester, and intimate with Turberville, the Hobys, and the Sidneys, was a member of the ambassadorial mission of Hoby to France at the time of the latter's death. He became an active Puritan writer. (*Certaine Tragicall Discourses*, Douglas edition, Introduction.)

1567	Bandello (fr. French of Boaistuau and Belleforest)	*Certaine Tragicall Discourses*	Lady Mary Sidney
1575	various authors	*Golden Epistles*	Anne (Cecil), Countess of Oxford

Edward Hake (fl. 1567-1588). For membership in Barnard's and Gray's Inns, see *Newes out of Powles Churchyarde*, "To the Gentle Reader." In 1585-1586 Hake became mayor of Windsor and in 1588 represented that place in Parliament. (Edmunds edition, p. xi.)

1579	author	*Newes out of Powles Churchyarde, a*	Earl of Leicester
1579 (1567?)		*Trappe for Syr Monye*	
1567	à Kempis	*Imitation of Christ*	Duke of Norfolk

Sir Christopher Yelverton (1535?-1612)

1572 (performed 1566)	author	*Epilogue to Jocasta*

Peter Beverley

1565/6?	founded on Ariosto	*Ariodanto and Ieneura*
1567	author	Verses in Fenton's *Certaine Tragicall Discourses*

[Humphrey] Cavyll (d. 1570)

1559	author	*Mirror for Magistrates* ("Mortimer")

INDEX